This book is

- you too have lived for a good many years, and would like to recall and share memories;

- you are younger in years, but fascinated by the happenings and the social changes since the mid-1900s;

- you share any of the interests of the author, such as travel, speaking and politics;

- you would like to discover a totally new structure for memoirs;

- or if you would simply like an enjoyable and very different read!

www.gwynredgers.com

Previous works by the same author are:

My Speaking Journey (2015)
Those Trinity Years (2016)

About the Author

The author, Gwyn Redgers, has enjoyed a long and interesting life. Born when George V was still king and Britain had an empire, he was at school during wartime and the Attlee years, and then progressed to National Service in Hong Kong and to University in Cambridge. He went on to have a long and successful marketing career, and also a long - though somewhat eventful - family life.

Finally came retirement, which has given him full scope for developing his interest in travel, his "speaking journey" and, most recently, his emergence as an author.

C'est la Vie describes 80 episodes of that 80 year life, some light-hearted, some serious, and all of them a stimulating read.

Or, as he himself puts it, the 'fun and follies of four-score years'.

Dedication

To my parents, who gave me the opportunities.

C'est la Vie

The fun and follies of four-score years

Gwyn Redgers

Published by
Filament Publishing Ltd.
16 Croydon Road, Beddington, Croydon,
Surrey, CR0 4PA, United Kingdom.
Telephone +44 (0)20 8688 2598
www.filamentpublishing.com

ISBN 978-1-911425-57-1

Table of Contents

Gwyn Redgers

1   **Prague Spring**

The occasion was a three-week tour with a friend Mark, then working in Nigeria, in which we were exploring Europe in his jazzy Scimitar sports car. We had started with the Oktoberfest in Munich, and had then travelled east behind the Iron Curtain. The year was 1968.

We reached the tiny square of the small town of Modry Kamen in Czechoslovakia in the early evening, and considered our plans. We needed petrol, a place to stay, and something to eat and drink. Then, while we were thinking, we were in for a surprise. Word had evidently got around that there was a car from England in town. This was novel. A figure appeared, flying down the small hill to where we were parked. As he ran, he was waving his arms and shouting (with an American twang to his accent) "God save the Queen, God dammit!"

He told us that his name was Gabor, and between the wars he had spent several years in Chicago. We enlisted his help, firstly with the question of locating a service station. As it happened, Gabor – who was seemingly aged about 60 – had a girlfriend working in a hospital in a village only a dozen or so miles away from where we were. Not exactly a service station, but he had a private arrangement for obtaining petrol. Problem solved – he would take us there.

The next problem was somewhere to stay. This too was easily solved. The kind lady who put us up for the night was Gabor's next-door neighbour. Finally came the question of food and drink. The number and location of refreshment establishments was largely decided by the regime. Two bars had been allotted to Modry Kamen, so we duly went to one of them. A simple meal was cooked for us and we spent the next two or three hours in imbibing the local schnapps. Incidentally this was called by everyone 'visky', regardless of its colour or its exact ingredients. The atmosphere was totally optimistic. Dubček was now the country's President and was introducing a more welcoming type of communism. And so the toasts flowed. Obviously to Dubček but also to Winston Churchill, to England, to America and so on (but not, I noticed, to Brezhnev). A particularly lively one was to 'Manchester United'.

One other problem successfully solved was the obtaining of more Czech currency. For this we had to thank Gabor's friend Stefan Strmy, who just happened to be the senior figure in the Communist Party locally. Mark had sensibly brought with him a quantity of US dollars. Stefan took us into a side room, locked the door, and duly transacted a currency exchange from US dollars into Czechoslovakian korunas.

The optimistic and always friendly atmosphere continued as we took the road towards Prague the following morning. Interest in our GB plates continued high and our car was at times applauded as we drove along. However at times we had to pull into the side of the road. This was to allow the passage of columns of Warsaw Pact tanks which were at that time streaming out of Czechoslovakia, back towards Russia. Eventually we arrived in the centre of Prague, Wenceslas Square, where we were able to talk to local students who also were totally optimistic about the Dubček regime. Prague itself was a delightful city. The only problem was that there was virtually nothing to buy with our newly acquired Czech currency. Then, from Prague, our trip continued – firstly northwards to East Berlin, and then through Checkpoint Charlie and back to England.

It was a fortnight later. I was at home, still thinking about the trip that we had made. I was very happy indeed for the Czechoslovakian people. Then came the shock. I turned on the radio. The main item on the BBC News was that Russia had arrested Dubček and that the Russian army was once again back in control of the country. C'est la vie.

2   My first trip abroad

I was 14 years old and the year was 1950 when I first went abroad. It was a school trip in which one of our teachers, Doc Collins, took a party of about 15 of us to Frankfurt am Main in the American Zone of Germany. This, I believe, was the first year in which ordinary travel to Germany was possible after the war.

It was a long journey. Firstly by train and then ferry to Ostend, then by train stopping at Maastricht and Aachen to Cologne, and finally down the Rhine heading towards our destination, Frankfurt. I retain my memories of that journey. For instance, it was the WVS, I believe, who provided refreshments when we stopped at Aachen, and also in the train as we travelled through the night was a small group on their way to Oberammergau for the 10-yearly festival.

My hosts were the family of 14-year-old Bernhard Moll who lived at Taunus Strasse, 29, close to Frankfurt's Hauptbahnhof. His father had returned home one year previously after wartime imprisonment in Yugoslavia. Frankfurt life was returning to normal. I was woken each morning at half past five by the relaying of the city's tram tracks outside my window. Also the famous Frankfurt book fair had just restarted. There was considerable war damage of course, but it seemed far less crippling in Frankfurt than that in Cologne, which we also visited, where the tall and beautiful Dom was about the only building still standing within an area of around half a mile on each side.

The welcome to our group of English schoolchildren was warm throughout. Perhaps more surprisingly, this warmth seemed to extend also to the members of the American occupying force walking around. It was indeed a case of "Wilkommen im Deutschland".

Let me mention just one memory that stands out. This was the day that Bernhard took me cycling to see something special about 10 miles south of Frankfurt. It was a wide and largely empty twin highway, totally remarkable and unlike anything I had ever seen before. It had been constructed by Germany's engineers shortly before the war, and was Germany's (and possibly the world's) first Autobahn.

It was some 20 years before that German innovation was to appear for the first time in Britain, in the shape of the Preston bypass.

3   Up Ramsey!

It was in 1963 that my wife Dickie and I first visited Northern Ireland. This was to stay for a week or two with friends Vera and Ted from Bedford, who were now living in Belfast. The IRA had called a halt to its slight earlier activity, and it was to be the year 1969 before "The Troubles" began. However the difference between the Catholic and Protestant communities in areas such as employment and living conditions was all too apparent.

Vera told us how her daughter had come back from her first day in her new school with a question, "Mummy, am I a Protestant or a Catholic?" The most accurate answer would have been "Neither", since neither Vera nor Ted had been near a church for many years. But an answer definitely had to be given, and they had settled for 'Protestant'.

The clear differences between the two groups was very noticeable as we went round the city. A huge wall painting of King Billy (that's William of Orange who defeated the ousted catholic King James II at the Battle of the Boyne in 1690) might dominate the end of a terrace of houses. Less visible, in the public toilets, the scribbles on the wall might well be praise or criticism, possibly of the Pope, or possibly of the Queen or even of the Archbishop of Canterbury who at that time was Archbishop Ramsey. I even remember seeing a biblical text from Hebrews written on a toilet wall, which was certainly a new kind of graffiti for me.

One interesting example of the problem occurred when Ted and I took ourselves off, over the Irish border, to beautiful Donegal for two days of sea fishing and camping. As we drove up to the border at Strabane, we noticed two or three groups of small boys assembled by the roadside. Then, as we actually entered the Republic, the first group yelled through our car window "Up the Pope!". Therefore, as we approached the next gang, I stuck my own head out first and shouted to them: "Up Ramsey!" The result was total bewilderment.

To me, a visitor to the six counties, it all seemed a game at that time – just local colour. How very different just five or six years later!

4   The Wartime Coconut

J ust picture it. A knock at the door. It was the postman, making a delivery. And the delivery? A coconut, with our name on it.

Picture it further. The year was 1942 or 1943. The middle of the war. Several years since anyone in Britain had seen a coconut.

But then this one actually appeared. The hair on part of the coconut had been carefully shaved off and on it was written in thick black ink "To Brian and Gwyn" and our full address in Potters Bar, plus an official-looking stamp.

The sender was our Auntie Lily. Before the war she had been an assistant matron at Barnet General Hospital. She had however signed up with QARANC – the Queen Alexandra's Royal Army Nursing Corps – and was currently serving in a military hospital located, I believe, in Jos in northern Nigeria. She herself was to go on later to serve in Burma and eventually in a field hospital in newly-liberated Austria. She sent my brother and me many letters during the war – censored of course – but never again anything so remarkable as that coconut.

Of course I took it to my primary school the next day, where it was a source of great wonderment to staff and pupils alike, earning me a host of brownie points. Then, two or three days later, we cracked it open. The milk inside it had dried up, but the taste of the fruit itself was excellent. As with other exotic fruits such as oranges and bananas, we had 2 or 3 more years to wait before coconuts would appear again in British shops.

5   King Zog

My father always enjoyed taking my brother and me to different interesting parts of London. For example he had got to know the Night Editor of the Daily Express and was able to take his sons along to Fleet Street, very late one evening, to tour the plant and see the paper being put to bed. On another occasion he arranged with a contact working at Tower Bridge for us to be able to visit and see the bridge actually being opened. And there were other visits too.

One particularly memorable occasion occurred when I was (I believe) eight years old in 1943. I remember being taken by my father one evening to Westminster to see Parliament in action. First of all, if I recall correctly, there was a two or three minute chat with our local MP. Following this we made our way up to a room adjacent to the Strangers' Gallery, as it was then called (now renamed the Visitors' Gallery). Inside there were two or three older men seated, including one who was clearly from a foreign country.

We made our polite introductions, conversed with them for a few minutes, and then all of us eventually went through into the Strangers' Gallery where we watched the debate taking place below us.

I have sat quite a number of times in the Strangers' Gallery since that date in 1943. The reason that I have always recalled this first visit to Parliament is the identity of that foreign gentleman, resident in Britain during the war, whom we talked with and sat next to that evening. It was in fact King Zog of Albania.

6   **War Graves**

The 20th century saw two world wars. Both included much fighting across the Channel in France and Belgium in which British soldiers took a leading part. Sadly, many thousands fell in battle, and their bodies have remained in war cemeteries – some of which I have visited – near where they fought and died.

My own first experience of war graves was at a time when a friend and I had set out on a cycling and camping holiday. It was well after dark on the first day, still in northern France, when we decided to stop and pitch our tent quite close to a roadside for the night. We slept well. However when we emerged from our tent in the light of the morning, to our surprise – and also to our horror – we were just yards away from an immense wartime cemetery containing row upon row of identical white crosses. Inadvertently we had chosen to camp in a location overlooking the cemetery. The nearby town was in fact Verdun, which remains to this day the principal field of wartime memory for all French citizens.

Another encounter took place about 30 years later. On that occasion my car had broken down on my way back to England, and I had left it for repair in the town of Cambrai in northern France. When I returned to Cambrai several days later and picked it up, I had several hours to kill before the time of my ferry.

I therefore took the opportunity to visit Ypres, just over the border in southern Belgium, where so much fighting had taken place in the First World War. There I was able to visit the Menin Gate – the memorial arch that carries many thousands of names of those British and Commonwealth soldiers who had died there in battle.

More especially, I was able to experience the ceremony which has taken place there every evening, apart from during wartime, in the century since those battles. A unit of four or five trumpeters from the town took up their position by the Menin Gate and played the last post, while other town dwellers and tourists watched and listened. It may have been commemorating the happenings of a hundred years ago, but it has remained intensely moving to this day.

7   With Jessica in Ireland

I have often said that I was married to a scooter.

Before and during my university years, I had no vehicle and no licence to drive one. But then Dickie, who was at that time doing her midwifery training at Cambridge's Addenbrookes Hospital, came into my life – along with her scooter, Jessica.

Jessica served us well for three or four years. The particularly memorable occasion which I am writing about today was when she conveyed us on a summer holiday to Ireland. The first few days were spent staying with a Dublin friend who was starting his television career with Telefís Eireann. Then followed a fascinating tour which included Waterford, Cork, Tipperary, Killarney, Limerick and the Dingle Peninsula. It was my first trip to Ireland, and was friendliness and *céad mile fáilte* all the way.

There were of course some very memorable moments. The opportunity to be dangled upside down from high up in a castle and to kiss the Blarney Stone. The tour of the Ring of Kerry and a nearby magical island. And our B&B landlady in Killarney who told us that her children learnt English at school and enquired whether the children in London were taught Irish.

It was at Inch on the Dingle Peninsula that we shared an evening in a pub with the members of a company who were filming a TV drama of "Playboy of the Western World" in the next village, and also held the following conversation with a local farmer. "My daughter is a nurse – a trained nurse. This week she is working as a – what do you call it? – a walk-on extra with that film company you will have seen on the strand. They are paying her the same as the other extras – and she's a fully trained nurse. Now that film (pronounced 'fill-erm') company comes from London. So you'll be knowing them. So can you go down there and do something about it?"

Jessica had indeed transported us to a very different world!

8   That 50 mile walk from Southend

Southend-on-Sea – but often rudely called Southend-on-Mud – is one of London's nearest and favourite seaside spots. I had been to it several times by train, bus or even cycling during my youth, and always enjoyed visiting the Kursaal, the Wall of Death and of course that exceptionally long pier and the small train which runs along it. However it was several years later that I enjoyed – or should I say succeeded in – making the 50 mile journey back from Southend to London on foot.

I was working at Bermondsey at the time as a Product Manager of Twiglets and sundry other Peak Frean biscuit brands when our Sports & Social Club decided to organise a night-time Charity Walk. This would be in aid of a new ward facility in London's Guy's Hospital. About 20 or 30 of us took part.

The walk started from Southend Pier at about midnight and, all being well, would end back in London at about lunchtime. I was looking forward to it. After all, once or even twice a year I would head north to the Lake District or perhaps Scotland for two or three days of fell-walking. A 50 mile walk along a flat highway to London should not be a problem. But I was to be proved wrong.

The night's first 20 or 30 miles to the outskirts of London were pleasant enough, but then, although I was wearing a good pair of walking shoes, the blisters began. I patched myself up with plasters, gritted my teeth and kept on walking. I was determined to succeed – and somehow I managed finally to limp through the gate of the playing field in South London which was our destination.

A night's sleep in my Fulham home, and the next day I visited the Accident & Emergency department of the small Chelsea Hospital. Even the experienced nursing staff marvelled at the extent of my blisters. "Why on earth did you undertake that walk?," asked a friendly doctor. "It was in aid of a new ward facility in Guy's Hospital", I replied. He looked at me sternly. "And then you had the nerve to come here, to this hospital, instead of to Guy's, to sort out the damage!"

I had no answer.

9   Spurs in School-Time

I have been a Tottenham Hotspur supporter for virtually the whole of my life. Why? Quite possibly because my brother, three years older than me, was an Arsenal supporter. That's the way it sometimes works with brothers!

My Saturday afternoon visits to their White Hart Lane ground were quite frequent from the age of 10 or 11 years onwards, and certainly in the early 50s when Spurs were at their peak, winning both league and cup. My school at that time was in Enfield which, in rail travel terms, was just 3 stations from White Hart Lane station in Tottenham. It was therefore not surprising that quite a number of my school friends should also be Spurs supporters.

As well as weekend matches, there were quite frequently mid-week matches within the football season. Nowadays these take place in the evening, under floodlights, but floodlighting for football did not exist in those years of the 50s. Instead the matches were held in the afternoon. Imagine – Spurs playing on a Wednesday afternoon – just three railway stations away. The temptation was too great.

As a sixth former, we had a few periods in the week which were for private study. I remember that these included Wednesday afternoons, which were partly intended for sports activity.

Unknown to the school authorities, some of us interpreted 'sports activities' as going illicitly to White Hart Lane. But was it unknown? Not completely.

One of the teaching staff of Enfield Grammar School at that time was Mr Low, the Music Master. I remember the first time that he and we almost bumped into each other at the Spurs ground on a Wednesday afternoon. We waited – but amazingly nothing was said. It happened on some further occasions too. I am pleased to say that he always kept our secret, and we always kept his. But maybe now, over 60 years later, it is safe to reveal the secret.

10   Olympics 1948

I was disappointed not to succeed in getting my requested Olympics Games tickets for here in Britain in 2012. But the demand for the events for which I applied was clearly too high, and I – like so many others – was forced to watch the excitement only on television.

However I had been to some Olympics events in London at an earlier time. The year was 1948. The war had ended three years previously. Holding the Olympic Games (they had not been held since 1936) was a sign that the world was getting back to normal. There were less sports represented than nowadays, but records were broken and personalities emerged. The names of such runners as Emil Zatopek and Fanny Blankers-Koen are unlikely ever to be forgotten.

The occasion which I shall never personally forget was the final day of the show jumping events. That was a sport that I had been totally unaware of, and in which the Britisher Harry Llewellyn, riding on Foxhunter, gained the Bronze Medal. The Harry Llewellyn/Foxhunter partnership went on to receive another medal – this time the actual Gold Medal – four years later as part of the British Show Jumping Team in the 1952 Olympics in Helsinki.

Another memory from those 1948 Olympics was of a different type. Within the boxing events, Britain had a winner named Johnny Wright, who won the middleweight Silver Medal. Some 15 or 20 years previously, he had been a wolf cub in the 1st Potters Bar Scout Troop, which met in the Scout Hut adjacent to my own house. Moreover the Cub Master at that time was my own father, and the friendship – though not a close one – continued to exist. Johnny Wright still lived in Potters Bar so, not surprisingly, we were able to meet up with him and chat for a time.

I am writing this when a further Olympic Games is taking place, this time in Rio de Janeiro. It still hurts me that I was unable to get a ticket when the Games were held in London 4 years ago, but that is what life can be like, and my great interest in the Olympics continues to this day.

11   Wicca World

I have been through various stages of religious experience, from my 'exclusive Plymouth Brethren' upbringing to the almost humanist world of Unitarianism currently. The three or four years I spent with Wicca back in my 30s were particularly enjoyable.

Leading the world of white witches in Britain at that time was Alex Sanders, who had appointed himself the title 'The King of the Witches'. He appeared from time to time both on TV and in the Press. Alex was both our teacher and, along with his wife Maxine, the practitioner. In the weekly meetings which we held in his Notting Hill flat, he both expounded the craft (as Wicca termed itself) to 15 or 20 of us, and led us through the many (unclothed) rituals. I still retain my copious notes, referred to as my 'Book of Shadows'.

At that time, I was renting a 2-up 2-down cottage in the small Northamptonshire village of Ringstead where the coven also assembled on occasions. The nearby quarries and copses gave us the opportunity of practising the rituals more realistically in the open air. I still have one cutting from the local Northamptonshire newspaper which reported the description given by one local boy who was hiding in a bush.

Particularly memorable was a trip which four or five of us took to Paris one weekend. The main purpose was to visit the Cathedral of Notre Dame and to conduct a brief (and clothed) ceremony in front of the statue of Joan of Arc, whom witches regarded as having been a particularly important leader of the craft. Fortunately no newspaper was present to record it!

There are of course numerous strands to paganism, for instance druidism, the Order of Deucalion, magical circles, and so on. There are too the groups, both here and around the world, whose witchcraft is certainly not at all "white". Is the world becoming more tolerant, I wonder? I ask this because the Daily Mail recently reported that "(prison officials) are handing out witches' wands, tarot cards and ceremonial robes to inmates who claim they are pagan".

12 With Swans Tours in Spain

I was fortunate enough to be a Spanish language student, seeking vacation work, at the time of the birth of the package tour industry. This was in the late 50s. The law which limited the overseas travel allowance to £25 had been repealed. Instead one or two forward-looking travel agencies – especially Swans Tours – had realised that there could be a mass-market looking to take their holiday abroad in the newly developing Costa Brava. "Holidays at prices you can afford – £35" stated the advert – and it worked. Travel would be by train and ferry, (air packages barely existed) and several thousands quickly took advantage.

It was the start of what later became referred to as Spain's '1000 miles of concrete'. Small fishing communities such as S'Agaro, San Feliu and Tossa de Mar blossomed into highly popular and prosperous resorts. In fact I recall one council official saying to me (jokingly) "If you give us Gibraltar, we will give you Tossa de Mar".

I would need to write a separate book to describe all my experiences as a Resident Representative in the Costa Brava and then for the next two years further south in Tarragona. The widespread idiosyncrasies of our tourists. Guiding groups to distilleries and to tourist sites. Taking groups to bullfights and even trying cape work in front of a charging animal myself (a cow, but still very frightening) in a village bullfight. Also attending one or two Catalan independence gatherings in what was still the Franco dictatorship.

The role of the rep was not just administrative. The basic aim was to give tourists the best possible time while they were on holiday in Spain. But in my final year I went a bit too far. Not only did I act as 'agent' for the local suppliers of coach trips, but I organised some of my own. This was not officially allowed at that time. I was duly reported to the authorities. My Swans Tours employers were tipped off, and I had to be 'smuggled' out of Spain by a different rail route.

But it had been good while it lasted.

13   A mother's interest

My mother always appeared to be a very reserved woman, not at all touchy-feely. I could not imagine her, for instance, ever mentioning matters sexual even remotely to her sons. In fact I recall once overhearing an off-the-cuff remark made by my father that, after the duty of producing two offspring had been accomplished, he and my mother had few if any further physical relationship moments.

Instead my mother's interests were almost entirely to do with motherhood and home management, which she carried out excellently. She was undoubtedly bright and intelligent, occasionally expressing regret that she had been removed from school by her guardian and put into service as a housemaid at 15, and that she had never had any career after her marriage. But, during the years that I was at school, she did have one strong interest that frequently took her out of the house. That, surprisingly, was professional cricket and in particular Middlesex Cricket Club.

The post-war years of the 40s were the time when cricket returned to its great popularity. Mum took us to see test matches at the Oval and at Lord's during those summers – the Victory Tests in 1945, India in 1946, South Africa in 1947 and Australia in 1948. Indeed I was in the crowd for Don Bradman's last test match, which took place at the Oval. We clapped the great man all the way to the wicket, then sat down in expectation for what we realistically felt might be another century. It was not to be. On the second or third ball that he received, he was bowled by Warwickshire's Eric Hollies, and we clapped him all the way back to the pavilion.

Apart from the test matches, those were the years – especially 1947 – in which Middlesex reached their glorious zenith. Robertson, Edrich, Mann, wicketkeeper Leslie Compton – all were highly talented. And among that special team, there existed in particular one player who we might now describe as 'cricket's national pin-up', but was then called 'the Brylcreem Boy' – Dennis Compton. He was indeed an exciting player to watch, as well as being a record breaker. His totals of 3816 runs and 18 centuries in the 1947 season have never been bettered. I'm extremely grateful to my mother for the many occasions in which she took us to Lord's to watch the all-conquering Middlesex side. They were wonderful days.

And now for an unexpected epitaph. My mother never lost her interest in cricket though she did not go to matches after her children grew older. In fact she was still a great supporter of Middlesex (and also of Southampton Football Club!) until the day she died. A few years after that sad day, I was browsing through some items of hers which had found their way into one of my archive boxes. There were several letters that she had received and also one that she had written but never posted. I took it out of its envelope and started reading. It began "Dear Dennis".

I think I'll leave it at that!

14   Start of the tech age

My career started in 1960, and it was only from about this date that having a computer started to be the norm for a company. It was likely to be found in the 'computer department', and be controlled by a specialist, whilst its use spread fairly quickly to different parts of the business, such as payroll or storage of stock.

Meanwhile, the existing methods of administration continued. For example I found, even at the end of the 60s, that the chief accountant of the firm in which I was working was still using an adding machine which he wound with a handle instead of a new-fangled electronic calculator. But then in the 80s came the 'one per desk' concept.

I first heard about this imminent plan from 'adopted daughter' Claudia's sister, Gerry, who was working for ICL at the time. Much smaller computers had now been invented, and ICL's intention was to persuade managers of departments to have their own calculating computer on their own desk. This was a revolutionary idea.

Meanwhile, quite separately, typewriters too were becoming electronic. It was in 1975 that I first experienced this. I was working in a life assurance company and it was an actuary who showed us his new toy one Friday afternoon. Several of us, including our typists, crowded into his office to see it.

What we were looking at was in fact one of the earliest floppy disk word processors. The days of Tipp-ex for correcting what you had typed were about to end. I remember the excitement of the typists when they saw it working. A year or two later, the typing function was transitioned into the computer instead of being developed separately. From then on innovation became even more rapid, both for the office and for individuals. Mobile phones. The World Wide Web. The Internet and emails. The explosion of social media. Technology has indeed altered the way we conduct our present and future life. And of course there is so much more to come before the robots finally take us over.

I should mention, by the way, that I have just dictated the above text to my computer via the wonder of voice recognition software.

15   Mr Webster

It was one summer Saturday that I decided to take my longest one-day bike ride. By this time I was very used to the daily 6-mile ride to school at Enfield and back, as well as cycling everywhere else in the north of London area. I was 12 or 13 at the time.

So I left home early on my Raleigh bike. A 3-speed gear, but no dropped handlebars. The weather was fine and I averaged around 13 miles an hour. I headed northwest, and after four or five hours I finally reached Stratford-upon-Avon. I had a quick look at the theatre and at Anne Hathaway's house, ate my sandwiches on the banks of the Avon, and all too soon it was time to start my journey back. This time I took a different route, heading down towards Wycombe before turning towards London.

It was whilst I was pedalling somewhere near Uxbridge that I started talking to a fellow cyclist. He was a friendly chap in his 40s whose name was Mr Webster. Very kindly, he invited me back to his house for a cup of tea. We chatted for about an hour. Then I said my goodbyes and set off again to cycle home before it became fully dark. I believe that I cycled for almost a hundred and twenty miles that day.

A journey like this was all totally normal for an active boy of my age at that time, with few cars on the roads. So why,

I wondered, when I told my mother about Mr Webster, did she seem somewhat anxious and in fact returned to asking about Mr Webster several times in the next few days? It all seemed most strange.

It was to be another 20 or 30 years before the concept of "stranger danger" was first voiced, and I was to have my answer.

16   Weeding between the lines

I started part-time working at the age of 12. It was not yet illegal at that age. My job was to do a paper round in Potters Bar for the local newsagent, Mr MacKenzie, who was a friend of my father. The work involved 7 early mornings a week, and this job lasted for several years. When I was 15, I believe, I became also able to work for the Post Office, delivering the Christmas mail in those hectic 3 weeks before Christmas Day. One final task before being called up for National Service in March 1956 at the age of 18 was a most interesting Christmas holiday job as a nursing orderly in the geriatric ward of a local hospital. There have of course been short-term periods of work since, such as 3 months of washing-up in a Champs Elysées restaurant and a brief period of teaching English in Madrid.

Nevertheless one of my most interesting paid activities was what a friend cynically referred to as "Weeding between the lines" for several months.

It was of course much more than that. The employer in question was an Irish firm, Tersons, based in North London, whose income came from providing gangs of labourers for maintenance work on the tracks of British Rail. The work varied considerably. On some days, it would really be no more than just sprucing up a section of track (hence the 'weeding between the lines' reference). At other times it was the heavy task of removing old rails and laying new rails in their place. Another frequent task was having to use shovels to unload full wagon-loads of stones or gravel. At times this could become competitive, with my Irish work-mates seeing who could unload a wagon in the shortest time.

The gang of which I was a member were all exceptionally friendly, mostly living or lodging in North London's Kentish Town or Tufnell Park, and sharing the same pubs in the evening. Also learning their names was no problem for me. 10 of the 12 were called Paddy, one was called Jock, and I was normally called Potters Bar!

Most of my subsequent working life took place in an office environment, far away from the world of manual labour. But the memory has never waned.

17   My earliest memory

I was three years and 11 months old. The afternoon was sunny and I was playing just outside the front door of our house 'Dulce Domum', 13 Quakers Lane, Potters Bar. The two earthenware pots of flowers had just been watered, because we were going away. The year was 1939 – September – and war had just been declared. My brother and I, together with my mother, were about to be 'evacuated' away from the London area. My father would be staying back in Potters Bar, from where he continued his job as a railway signalman. Our destination was to be the home of Mr Norris, another member of the Plymouth Brethren community, who lived in the small village of Cam in Gloucestershire.

We were waiting for Mr Dimory to come in his car – a Lanchester, I believe. When he arrived, we loaded up our suitcases and some games and my teddy bear Rupert, and set off. By early evening we had reached Northleach where we stopped for a break at Home Farm, which was the dwelling of some other community friends, finally reaching Cam as it was getting dark.

I was happy to stay with Mr Norris. He had a pleasant garden with chickens and some fruit trees, and worked every day at Cam Mill about a mile away. On the other side of the road where he lived was a LMS railway branch line, running from

Coaley Junction to the small town of Dursley, on which the 'Dursley Donkey' passenger train ran three or four times a day. And just a few hundred yards away was a local hill which bore the name of Cam Peak.

Back in Potters Bar, despite the declaration of war, all was quiet. The anticipated bombing never transpired. Invasion did not seem to be expected. So why were we staying in Cam? After just eight or nine months, we therefore moved back to our own home in Potters Bar.

We were just in time for the start of the Blitz.

18   Genoa

The city of Genoa has played a large part in my life in recent years. It started with my meeting with Mark Covell – known to all of us Sky - who became one of the best-known of the many victims of the violence meted out by the Italian police after the G8 week of protests in 2001. Battered into a 2-day coma despite the fact that his 'crimes' were being a computer journalist, Sky finally received sizeable compensation after eight years, and was also awarded the Citizenship of Genoa by the City's Mayor.

But all that is his story, which I hope that one day he may write. Meanwhile it was also my introduction to a part of my life in which I visited Genoa with Mark several times.

My memories are strong. For instance there were the people I met. I remember with pleasure the two or three evenings I spent as a guest of Heidi whose son Giuliano was actually shot by the police as he was protesting. Partly in recognition of her loss, the people of Genoa elected Heidi to the Italian Parliament, and she spent several years in Rome. There was Enrico Zucca, the Genoese prosecutor who did not believe the story fashioned by Silvio Berlusconi and his Deputy Gianfranco Fini, but carried out his own researches, partly with Sky's aid. Sincere and gentle, and a practising Buddhist himself, he finally achieved complete success for Sky and other victims in his prosecutions. Then there was

Graziella, another member of Parliament herself, who was my companion in the courthouse on the day that a police appeal was partially granted to the cries of 'Vergogna, Vergogna' (shame) by all those present. Fortunately the final stage of Italy's 3-stage legal process later overturned that disappointing second stage verdict.

Most of all I remember Teresa and her husband Giorgio from the nearby township of Pugli who had taken excellent - almost motherly - care of Sky over the many years when he was fighting the case, and who was my hostess whenever I was in Genoa myself.

I could go on to talk more about Genoa. About the city itself, from the ferry and the fascinating port to the narrow streets and many historic buildings. About the visit to the Diaz school where the police violence had actually taken place. Meeting and talking with the filmmaker Domenico Procacci, a winner at an earlier Berlin Film Festival, whose film of the event ('Diaz – Don't clean up this blood') would be shown all over Italy. And that day of the final court victory, and the celebration that followed. Plus of course the fact that at some time during those 10 years of court struggle, Sky met the very lovely Laura.

Genoa has indeed been a special place. For me, this is because of my visits there over these last 10 or 15 years. And for Sky, not only for that terrible incident and long legal struggle, but because during that time he met Laura and they now live happily together.

19   Church visiting

It gives me great pleasure that, despite the risk of severe injuries or even death, commuting by cycling has returned so strongly within the London area. In fact a dedicated cycling highway right along the Thames from east to west is envisaged. But it is of course most unlikely that the practice of cycling will return to the pre-eminence it had in those days before car ownership was universal.

For me, up to the age of 20 or thereabouts, cycling was my normal method of transport, especially as my parents never owned a car. I would regularly cycle to school, to the nearby villages and towns in Middlesex and Hertfordshire, and even at times to central London. Then too "behind the bike sheds" was seen in every school as a classic place for trysts to occur.

One quite frequent activity that I look back on with great pleasure were the rides I took with my school friend Laurence Turner around the ages of 10 and 11, when we were still in primary school. Our purpose in these rides was first and foremost to discover and visit village churches in Hertfordshire and Essex. This was not for any religious reason. Instead it was a mixture of local history and architectural appreciation. For centuries, the church had been central to every village and town. The record of those years could be read since, in nearly every case, we would find a brief printed history within even the smallest parish church. Externally every church would have its own architectural character, for example a tower or spire, and an array of buttresses and gargoyles, plus quite possibly an interesting churchyard. Within the building there would be different styles of chancel and occasional chapels, together with a variety of monuments in stone or brass. At times, if no adult was present, I might even try out the organ.

Additionally there were the larger churches, such as Waltham or St Albans Abbey to visit and study, plus numerous other interesting and very old buildings in the villages that we passed through. Then too we could also discover new towns such as Stevenage and Harlow being built.

I cannot claim that this interest and the places we visited were particularly exciting, neither can I report that any particular incidents stood out. Looking back, however, I enjoyed those rides with my friend Laurence. It was certainly a most interesting activity of my childhood, and worth recording just for that reason.

20   A brief memory of bombs

Come, friendly bombs, and fall on Slough!
It isn't fit for humans now,
There isn't grass to graze a cow.
Swarm over, Death!

John Betjeman, 1937

I am writing this at a time when wars, senseless killings and civil unrest are happening in many countries in the world. We in the United Kingdom are grateful that we have been spared this in our own country. The last experience of such violence was in the 80s when the IRA was at its most active. We had for instance the explosions in the Grand Hotel in Brighton, in those pubs in Birmingham, and the attacks on London's Underground and on the Horseguards exercising in Regents Park.

I have just one personal incident to report from that time. It was during the morning after the Brighton explosion that Dickie, my ex, chose to park her car on a yellow line directly outside the Millbank Tower close by Parliament. She was possibly the only person in the country who had somehow missed hearing about the previous day's explosion. When she came back, she found that her car had been cordoned off by the police. Unable to get back to her car, the nearest policeman explained, "Keep back from that car, madam. the bomb squad is on its way". Calling out the bomb squad for her parking offence? Dickie was having none of it. She slipped under the ropes, ignored the shouts of the police, ran to the car, got in, and drove quickly away.

For actual experience of explosive weaponry, I have to go back to wartime itself. Potters Bar, being outside London's Green Belt, was far enough away from the centre of London to luckily avoid the Blitz. We were very aware of it of course, both from the BBC's broadcasting, and through being able to see that red glow in the sky night after night as we looked from our slightly higher altitude towards London itself. Also, if we stayed the night with our relations near Archway, we might have to bed down on a London Underground platform. Then later on in the war, I remember at least two occasions when the drone of a doodlebug flying overhead suddenly stopped, and we ran for cover.

But Potters Bar did not completely escape the wartime bombing. In fact we did have a landmine and 3 bombs (I believe) early in the war, and one V1 doodlebug and one V2 rocket later in the war. One of the bombs demolished a house just opposite my primary school, whilst another caused much damage in the small road where my grandmother lived. However it was the V2 rocket that I most remember.

It was a Saturday afternoon and I was in the garden when we heard an almighty explosion. Several panes of glass in our greenhouse suddenly cracked. Automatically my brother and I grabbed our bikes and cycled off to find what had happened. We found that a V2 had actually fallen on Southgate Road which was about a mile away. Emergency services were already at the site, and we were not allowed to get too near. I can still partly picture the scene, but the main reason why it stays in my memory is that it had demolished the house of a school friend, Alistair Pigden. Very sadly his brother was at home, and was killed.

We in Potters Bar got off extremely lightly compared with many other locations. However the memory has never departed, and I sincerely hope that this type of incident will never again happen in our country.

21   Chase Farm Hospital

Chase Farm Hospital in Enfield is currently commencing a 2-year development programme. Hearing this news recently took me back to events in my earlier life.

The first of these events was when, at the age of 7 years, I had cycled with my older brother one morning the 20 miles from Potters Bar to St Albans and back. Then, that afternoon, I went to play in what we called at the time "the field" which was in fact a part of my road where houses had not yet been built. Instead, as well as trees and grass, it held a small underground bunker fully protected by coils of barbed wire.

One of the great pleasures of my life was climbing trees. That afternoon I went a stage too far, and a branch that I was standing on snapped. I landed heavily inside that barbed wire enclosure. Somehow I scrambled through, and returned home somewhat tearful and with clear signs of a broken arm. An ambulance was called, and transported me to a ward within Chase Farm Hospital, some 6 miles away. Everyone was most friendly and the operation promised to be straightforward, but then it all changed. One of the nurses, presumably unaware of why I was in the hospital, yanked me up by my arms in bed, and a simple break turned into a compound fracture. I still bear the 22 stitches of the operation which resulted.

The second event concerning Chase Farm was some 10 years later when, as a sixth-former, I worked for some three weeks before Christmas on the hospital's male geriatric ward. It was an eye opener for me. On one hand, I had my first contact with colostomy bags, with such conditions as cancer and Parkinsons, and with the very end of life. On the other hand I was able to experience and appreciate for the first time the knowledge, skills, friendliness and dedication of nursing and medical staff. This is something that I feel strongly about right to this day.

I have written elsewhere of 'My Health Story' and my appreciation of the remarkable work of the NHS. I certainly wish the very best for the 'new look' Chase Farm Hospital that will be appearing in two years time.

22 Stonehenge

It has never been easy to find a virgin when you need one – not that that is frequent.

Writing about Stonehenge takes me back to my army life. Naturally the memories which stand out mainly refer to those one and a half years I spent serving Her Majesty in Hong Kong. But I recall too the initial six months which were spent in this country, training for what was to follow.

The first month was spent at Oswestry, going through that process known as square-bashing. Another name for this would be bullying, applying for instance to one's well groomed hair being mercilessly cut off, and spending some of one's nights bulling or shining your boots rather than enjoying some well-earned sleep. Mind you, the process had its point. The task of the NCOs was to ensure that every soldier would respond unquestioningly to every order, no matter how absurd, and this was largely achieved by shouting at you from a distance of 3 inches.

From Oswestry I proceeded to a Royal Artillery camp at Tonfanau on the Welsh coast, which had the redeeming feature that it was very handy for climbing up Cader Idris mountain. I was posted from there on to Larkhill camp on Salisbury Plain, which also had a redeeming feature. That feature was its nearness to Stonehenge.

And so it happened that, as dawn broke on the longest day of the year, i.e. 21st June in 1954, three or four of us squaddies from the camp just a mile away were at Stonehenge and able to marvel at the accuracy of the timing when the rising sun shone light on the Heel Stone of that ancient monument. Only a few outside visitors were present – Stonehenge was not sealed off by fencing in those days – and the Druids had wisely postponed their own ceremonies to the next day apparently to avoid the 'crowds'.

As native Britishers we decided that it would be right and proper to perform our own sacrifice to celebrate this special event. The only thing missing was a virgin to sacrifice. The nearest that we got to the real thing was a Year One female undergraduate from Bristol University. She was quite happy to claim virginity and to lay down with legs and arms extended on the appropriate ancient stone.

And the sacrifice itself? What happened? I leave that to your imagination!

23 Zeppelin

Nowadays there is no such animal as a non-combatant.
Modern warfare is total warfare.
Peter Strasser, Führer der Luftschiffe 1916-1918
(Leader of Airships)

am sure that every home in the country has at least one relic from the past. In my case, one of my relics is a 3-foot ong metal fragment that is in fact a piece of a First World War Zeppelin.

The Great War was the first time when aerial warfare made ts appearance. Almost unbelievably for the British public to imagine, German Zeppelins appeared over London and several other East Coast towns such as Hartlepool, and even dropped bombs. But then came some relief in the shape of the newly formed Royal Flying Corps. The key moment in London was when Squadron Leader Leefe Robinson of the newly-formed Royal Flying Corps shot down a Zeppelin early in 1915. The place was Cuffley, just north of London.

The public interest was intense. In fact many Londoners made a special journey from Kings Cross to Cuffley by train to see the wreck of the Zeppelin on the ground. Clearly it had to be guarded and kept safe from souvenir hunters. And who better to do it than police officers from Y Division in north London? Amongst these was my grandfather, who thereby spent two or three weeks at the scene keeping the wreckage safe from mischievous hands

So how, we must wonder, did a piece of First World War Zeppelin arrive in grandfather's house in Little Heath, then in my father's house in Potters Bar, and finally in my own home?

We can only ponder how this strange and even illegal event might have happened. I myself can only say "Thank you, grandpa".

24   My first discovery of Spain

I would sooner be a foreigner in Spain
than in most countries.
How easy it is to make friends in Spain

George Orwell

Spain was to figure frequently in my life. It started when, as a 5th former, I and several others were allowed to add a further language to our studies. This was Spanish. We learnt it partly from a French language teacher, Mr Hudson, who taught us from the front of the grammar book while he himself was learning from the final pages. We were also to share some lessons with a more experienced teacher in the neighbouring Enfield County Grammar School for girls.

In fact it was she who suggested that I might go in August 1952 to attend a fortnight's Spanish teaching class to be held by Liverpool University's Professor Allison Peers in San Sebastian in Northern Spain. My parents agreed, and the course fee, some spending money, plus the return rail ticket from London to San Sebastian were forthcoming.

The fortnight passed quickly and proved most useful and enjoyable. One of the highlights was a trip to Pamplona, which was famous for the running of the bulls. Another was more political in nature. In those days, the Spanish government operated from San Sebastian rather than from Madrid during the summer months. I remember standing in the portal of San Sebastian's Cathedral when two people pushed past me. One of these was wearing army uniform. It was in fact the only time when I actually came into touching contact with Generalissimo Franco, the Caudillo of Spain.

At the end of my two week course, I still had about £10 left. I was therefore able to buy what was known as a kilometric rail ticket for £4, which took me nearly the whole way round the country. In particular my itinerary included Madrid, Toledo, Cordoba, Seville, Granada and Alicante. The ticket finally ran out in Burgos where I had the nerve and the good fortune to ask a visiting English couple to lend me the money to complete my journey back to San Sebastian (where my return ticket to London would commence).

Goodness knows how I survived. Sleeping was normally on a train or in the open air. Drink was mainly water. Food was largely bread and picking every type of fruit. All this was necessary, since my money was needed to pay for admission fees in every place which I visited. Nevertheless my memories of this first voyage of discovery through Spain have always remained etched in my mind. Here are two of them.

My last port of call was to a small township just outside Alicante, which was the home of Isolina Sevila who was the pen-friend of my fellow Enfield sixth former, Peter Ottino.

Thanks to Christmas cards and just two or three visits, my friendship with Isolina was to last for the next 50 years!

Finally, if I were asked to pick one particular highlight out of many, it would be standing on the Albaicin hill in Granada, viewing the Alhambra by moonlight, and being invited into a gypsy's cave – completely gratis – to enjoy a friend-and-family evening of flamenco.

Spanish episodes are bound to crop up again in this volume of memoirs, but this is how it all started.

25 A Bournemouth memory

'You have to try everything once' is a well known rule of life. Rather less well-known is the statement 'You have to try everything in life once – except for sky diving', but that is another story.

I recall that I was carrying out my National Service at the time that "once" happened for me. On this occasion, a 36 hour leave had enabled me to go down in civvies from my Salisbury Plain camp to enjoy the sea at Bournemouth. My weekly 24 shillings army pay packet certainly did not stretch to a hotel, but I was comfortable enough sleeping in a deck chair in a secluded spot just off the main promenade.

It was about 11 PM that a middle-aged guy came up to me and started chatting. He found out that I was a soldier and remarked that he had spoken to several soldiers and they were friendly. Friendly? Somehow his hand brushed against my trousers and I understood what 'friendly' meant. One classmate had in fact described these types of actions to some of us, though only in words.

I realised very quickly that I was not expected to do anything myself. Instead his hand began to brush me more insistently. Finding no objection, the hand finally groped inside my trousers and – surprise surprise – found and brought out a penis. Then came the rubbing. At the same time, he brought out his own penis and rubbed that too. There were certainly strong sensations and within a very few minutes we both ejaculated. Apparently this was all. He gave me the briefest of kisses and went on his way.

Yes, one should be prepared to try everything once. But although I have the greatest respect for the many gay friends whom I have made during my lifetime, I found no particular pleasure in what took place that evening, and have had no wish to repeat the experience.

26   My night inside

For several months of my military service in Hong Kong, I was moved from my 'surveying' role in 197 Locating Battery on the island to a desk job with a different responsibility at Garrison HQ on the mainland in Kowloon. The task was to administer Operation Charlotte. Briefly, this was to maintain a list of addresses of all service families in the Colony, and thus to be able to arrange for a swift evacuation of all if strife should break out. I found this an interesting role. One of the advantages was that it was nearer to the church which I was attending and helping on the mainland.

It all seemed so straightforward. But trouble erupted.

I was leaving Garrison HQ for church one evening when the staff sergeant on duty at the gate decided that he should look at the papers that I was holding. To my horror, some of what I had been writing for the church meeting was on the back of Operation Charlotte instructions. His response was immediate. Two Military Police were immediately called. A personal search. Then a forced quick-march through the barracks and (clearly visible to all looking on) to the Guard Room. A further search. The removal of my trousers. And a night sleeping on bare boards.

In the morning I was force-marched again, this time to the office of the Camp Commandant. Some questioning, and then a return to my imprisonment in the Guard Room. During the day I was twice interviewed by a junior officer from the Intelligence Corps.

It did not take too long to reach a conclusion of my case. They clearly saw me as a most careless soldier, but not as a spy. Also, disappointingly, I was immediately relieved of my duties concerning Operation Charlotte and returned to my former occupation in Leymun camp on the Hong Kong island.

This episode was clearly a black mark on my military record and would have prevented any advancement. Thank goodness that I had no ambitions of that type.

27   Fyfe Robertson in Bedford

One of the mainstays of the BBC television schedule back in earlier days was the "Tonight" programme. It was led by Cliff Michelmore, and one of the most distinctive contributors was the Scotsman, Fyfe Robertson, wearing his Sherlock Holmes-style headgear. He fronted a wide variety of stories. Thus it was no surprise that he should visit Bedford to discover the facts behind the many local complaints about Italian immigrants who had come quite recently to work in the brickworks.

Bedford was my wife Dickie's home town. We arrived one evening for an overnight visit to her parents and were immediately told the full story by mother Thea and by father Bill. Bill had been on his way home when he had been stopped in the street by a stranger who asked him where all the Italians were living. Bill's response to the stranger's question had been "Aren't you Fyfe Robertson?" That having been agreed, Bill invited him back to his house to hear all about the terrible Italians from Thea. The result of her discussion with Fyfe Robertson was that it was agreed that a BBC camera crew would come round to the street in the morning, and that an interview would take place.

The morning arrived, as did the BBC camera crew and Fyfe Robertson. He started by briefly outlining the complaints being made in Bedford about their new Italian residents.

Then turning to Thea, he stated: "Mrs Blades. I know that you feel strongly about these new arrivals and how they are affecting all of your lives. Please tell us about it." Then Thea started. "Yes, there's quite a lot of talk about them but they're not really so bad", and so on, and so on. To which Fyfe Robertson, after only a few further seconds, called out smartly "Cut!"

He turned to Thea. "Mrs Blades, is that your daughter and her husband standing over there?" "Yes" she replied. Fyfe Robertson continued. "Did they come up from London to see you last night?" "Yes", replied Thea. "And did you discuss all about the fact that you would be talking on television about the Italian issue in the morning?" Again the answer was "Yes" from Thea. "Well, Mrs Blades," responded Fyfe Robertson sternly, "they've come up from London and people think differently there. Now you live here in Bedford, which is where these Italians are living, and I want you to tell us what you and all the other people in Bedford really think. Will you do that?" "Yes", said Thea, and the cameras restarted.

"Now I have with me from Bedford Mrs Blades who feels quite strongly about the arrival of these Italians. Mrs Blades, please tell us what you think." And Thea was off. "They make so much noise till very late every night, and it used to be a quiet street. Then their children seem to be quite out of control for much of the time. And they hang sheets out of windows and even hang mattresses at times. And there are other things too. They started an Italian club in that building on the corner. It's terrible here now. We just don't like it".

There is no doubt that it was an excellent interview. We went back to London that afternoon and met a friend who happened to comment, "Did you hear that dreadful woman going on about Italians on the television earlier today?"

And back in Spencer Road in Bedford? The conversation between all the bystanders, both English and Italian people, continued after the BBC contingent left. Bill and Thea were invited to that new Italian club the following evening, and peace, harmony and friendship were established for ever more.

28   Friends of Chilonga

M argaret had been a VSO (Voluntary Services Overseas) worker, based in a hospital in Chilonga in Zambia, during the worst time of the AIDS epidemic. She had seen for herself a generation of parents dying with AIDS, and thus the orphan children left in the care of grandparents and needing to be used to till the land. On her return to the UK, to her home in our village of Winchcombe, she was determined to do what she could to help.

The need she identified was for education – not at primary level, which was free – but at secondary level, which would cost a child about £5 a month and was therefore totally unaffordable for the mass of villagers. Having secondary education was vital if the problems caused by AIDS were ever to be solved.

So what could we do? Our answer, after discussion, was to set up a fundraising Trust, and thus the Friends of Chilonga was born. The mechanisms were created. On one hand was a small Board of Trustees of which I was Chairman. On the other hand was a slightly larger committee to carry out the fundraising activities. It was indeed an English village's response to the huge problem faced by some villages in Zambia.

The elements clicked into place. Leaflets and posters. An artist-created logo. Collecting tins. A table and display at the annual village fairs. The strong support of Winchcombe's vicar, Rev. Michael Page, who felt strongly that his church should have one or two special causes to support.

There was unexpected help too. On one occasion a Roman Catholic nun, who hailed from the Chilonga area, came and gave a talk about the AIDS crisis to the Anglican church congregation. Few who were present will ever forget the day when a practising nun explained to them the mechanism of 'dry sex' which was used widely in sub-Saharan Africa and which contributes greatly to the way in which AIDS spreads there.

With Margaret's drive and contacts, the Zambian procedures also took shape. The local diocese was happy to allot the money we collected to local secondary schools in return for their promise to recruit pupils based on that money. Most importantly, a local man – Albert – was appointed to keep closely in touch with each school and thus avoid that major problem, seemingly endemic in Africa, where charity money goes sadly "adrift".

The results were impressive. A year after launch, Margaret made a return visit to Chilonga and was able to report back to us on a large rise in secondary school population. This number grew into the hundreds, and after only four or five years the first one or two undergraduates emerged from the schools and could be funded.

Many good initiatives come to an end, however, and this was the case with the Friends of Chilonga. The reason was a sad one. The Trust's man on the ground in Chilonga, Albert, on whom so much depended, contracted AIDS and very quickly could not continue. Trustee discussions were held, and the matter was also discussed with the local diocese and with the Catholic charity, CAFOD. Zambia was now much more geared up to supporting education than in those earlier years, and CAFOD as well as the local diocese were well represented on the ground. Thus a decision was reached to transfer the work of the Friends of Chilonga to CAFOD who would carry it forward.

It was a difficult decision to take, however we felt it was for the best. But, as mentioned above, those involved will never forget those Friends of Chilonga days, especially that day when a nun explained in detail the mechanisms of dry sex to Winchcombe's church congregation.

29   Nelson Mandela

used to say that I had one principle in life. That principle
was never to buy anything from South Africa. The reason
was my total hatred of apartheid.

This principle was severely tested in the year 1977 when
I moved to the Cotswolds and joined the company
Schlesinger Life, later to be renamed Trident Life. It had
in fact been founded by a South African and still retained
some links. However by this time it was completely British.

During those years, the man who was to really personify the
South Africa situation was serving 27 years of imprisonment
on Robben Island. This was Nelson Mandela. However the
campaign to release him (and of course to end apartheid)
was gradually building strength. Finally, in 1990, came that
occasion that we all remember when Nelson Mandela
walked free from jail. Then came those remarkable years
of vindication when he showed the world the strength of
his ideals. Policies such as the Truth and Reconciliation
Commission under the inspiring leadership of Archbishop
Tutu remain an example to follow for all the world's
countries. And who will ever forget that television occasion
when President (by this time) Mandela expressed his huge
joy at his Rainbow Nation's all-white team winning the
Rugby World Cup in South Africa itself?

A special occasion for me was the day when Nelson Mandela was due to speak to a British crowd in Trafalgar Square from the balcony of South Africa House. I was by this time a Londoner again. Unfortunately I was suffering from a bout of bronchitis, but of course I dragged myself from my bed of sickness and joined the welcoming crowd that had gathered to see and hear him.

It was whilst we were waiting for him to appear on the balcony that a French television crew came up to our section of the crowd and asked if any of us spoke French. I responded in the affirmative, and found myself explaining in French, on camera, for two or three minutes what Nelson Mandela meant to me and to the whole British nation. All in all, it was a great day to remember.

30   **Coronation**

Nowadays most celebrations are viewed on television. However I have always enjoyed seeing them in person, and London provides many opportunities. For example, each year gives an opportunity to stand by the roadside and watch the Lord Mayor's Procession or, at times, the Easter Parade, whilst at various times in the past (but not recently) I have travelled over to Tottenham to see the celebration when my football team wins the FA Cup or the League. However those I chiefly remember tend to be this country's Royal events.

It was in 1953, one year after ascending the throne, that the Queen had her Coronation. I came up to town with my friend Janet the evening before, with sleeping bags, and we joined the throngs who were already present in the Mall. The day started early for all of us. First to arrive were the cleaning battalions, who received great roars of applause. Then, during the next two or three hours, the marching started. First came units of soldiers who lined the road. Shortly after numerous police also marched up and down the roadside.

Then, whilst we all continued to wait, an item of news was excitedly passed from ear to ear throughout the whole crowd. Mount Everest had finally been climbed, by a New Zealander and a Sherpa! Could the day be any better than this, we wondered?

Then, at the appointed late morning time, came the procession that we were all waiting for. As we looked back down the Mall towards the Palace, line after line of foot soldiers and cavalry came into view and passed smartly by, and the air was filled with the music of the military bands. Following them came the state coaches themselves, both open and closed, each with its horses and footmen, and each containing Commonwealth leaders or the United Kingdom's own nobility.

Some we could recognise – others we couldn't. One of the latter has passed into history. This was the open coach containing a small middle-aged male figure and the very voluminous Queen of Tonga. It was Noel Coward who, when asked who was the male figure in the coach, replied that it was the Queen of Tonga's breakfast.

But back to the main purpose of the day, I can still feel the excitement all around me as the sumptuous coach carrying the Queen and the Duke of Edinburgh passed by. It was a truly remarkable day and, of course, later in that day that majestic procession once again passed by on its way back to Buckingham Palace, where a balcony appearance took place.

I was totally unaware at the time that my future wife Julie was camped almost directly opposite where I was standing in the Mall. Many years later, however, we were together in that same stretch of road to see the royal wedding of Prince Charles and Diana. Once again the same routines of staying overnight and applauding the cleaners in the morning. Once again the military processions, the musical fanfares and the long line of state coaches. It was the passage of Diana with her father on their way to St Paul's that of course gained the greatest cheer on that occasion.

By this time, television was in full ascendancy and we were able to view the events of the whole day on returning home. Little did we know then that only a dozen or so years later the Mall and Westminster Abbey would need to host one of the saddest processions of my life, which was Diana's funeral cortège. I was not present in person that day but viewed it on television.

2015 and 2016 have seen numerous ceremonial occasions in London. My closing wish is that long may they – and the Queen – continue to flourish.

31   Collecting bug

Where does a collecting bug begin? I have a friend whose husband's collection of dragons extends all over their house, and another who has proudly amassed no less than 100 copies of Wisden, the cricketer's annual bible.

My own early years were spent 'spotting' locomotive and bus numbers, which was a hobby that I shared with my older brother Brian. It started at around the age of eight years, and both Brian and I took our turns at running the 'Spotters Club' at our grammar school. To this day, I retain my collection of Ian Allan spotters guides, with their host of underlined bus or engine numbers. In fact it is hard to pass 280 Vauxhall Bridge Road without recalling the meetings of fellow spotters that were held by Ian Allan himself at that office address. But time passes. I retain much interest in our transport systems, but not that of a collector.

Another interest, quite possibly dating from the same age of 8 or thereabouts, was stamp collecting. Here a group of 4 or 5 of us were encouraged by our 'church elder', Mr Bull, who worked in the international company Cable and Wireless. About twice a year he passed on to us large numbers of stamps that had been taken from the envelopes of that company's correspondence.

My own collection grew steadily. The most exciting time was my schoolboy visit to Frankfurt-am-Main in 1950 where I was able not merely to obtain numerous stamps of the American, British, French and Russian post-war administrations of Germany, but also many 1,000,000 Mark or similar banknotes from Germany's cash crash of 1926.

I ceased collecting after my teenage years, but retained the albums. It was thus a terrible shock some 20 or so years later to discover that they had been stolen. My reaction was to completely restart my philatelic collection, this time concentrating strongly on the Balkans and South America, and limiting myself to stamps issued no later than 1950. But my interest fell away during recent years, and I eventually sold my collection to a dealer (for just a small profit) two years ago.

Another symptom of my 'collecting bug' disease, back in my youth, was that I created my own fairly small collection of moths and butterflies, and even (I shamedly have to admit) raided bird nests from time to time. However these were passing stages. They did not outlast my school years, and another collecting interest took its place.

It was eventually books which formed the main subject of my own collecting bug.

It started in quite a normal way. I enjoyed reading. Also, as my studies of French and Spanish progressed, I started to collect the old masterpieces written in those languages.

One has to remember there were no computers or 'Google Search' possibilities for many years to come.

Another source of book buying over many years was jumble sales and occasionally old bookshops. I had no particular collecting plan in mind – just whatever was available for a few pence (in those days) that took my fancy. The nearest thing to a collection turned out to be obtaining no less than 60 of Agatha Christie's works. More seriously, I did attempt to have one title – occasionally more – of all principal literary figures.

In the end it turned out to be lack of book shelf space which put the end to this particular collecting bug, but not before I had reached and catalogued almost 4000 titles. Only a handful of these have any financial value, and that purely by accident, e.g. the discovery that some of my purchases turn out to have been first editions.

And what of their future? In olden days, a collection of 4000 books might well have seemed something of an achievement or even an investment. Now, unfortunately, there has been the invention of the kindle. But in the meantime they continue to give me pleasure.

32 A job in the Bunny Club

No one ever believes me when I tell them that I was offered a job in the London Bunny Club. But it's true. Here is the story.

My first job on leaving university was exactly what I was wishing for. This was a graduate traineeship with a leading advertising agency, Erwin Wasey, whose client list at that time included many household names such as Coca-Cola, Procter & Gamble, Hoover and Quaker. During my seven years with the firm, I spent two years in its Bureau of Commercial Research (gaining knowledge of which was to prove invaluable in the latter stages of my career) and three or four years in the growing field of 'marketing'. My experience included being responsible for an innovative New Product Workshop, whilst I and a colleague together wrote what would have been the first British book on 'new product development'. Unfortunately he left to start his own business before we had entirely finished the last chapters, the writing ceased, and we had to return our advanced royalty cheque to the publishers, Harraps.

However it was time for me also to move on from agency life to 'client side' life. Marketing, by now firmly established in consumer markets, was my preferred way ahead.

Amongst the offers which I found advertised was one from Associated Biscuits Ltd, which was a company comprising Peak Freans, Jacobs and Huntley & Palmer. The firm's need was for a further product manager. Interestingly the selection method included their inviting a shortlist of 5 applicants to come together for an evening discussion about a possible new product campaign. I found this enjoyable and felt that I contributed quite well. The next day my office telephone rang. It was the Marketing Manager of Associated Biscuits, phoning from the Reading Head Office. He would like to meet me for lunch in London. And the place? Very surprisingly, the venue would be the restaurant of the Playboy Club, which had been established a year or so earlier, just off Park Lane.

It was a very pleasant lunch, even though I was somewhat distracted by the semi-nudity and the fluffy ears of those who served us. We shared a few moments of small talk, and my host then offered me the position of Product Manager of children's, cream and savoury biscuits (including Twiglets), which I happily accepted.

. . . . . And if that is not "being offered a job in the Bunny Club", then I'll eat my hat!

33   **Suez Crisis**

So this was it. My three years at university were finally starting.

It had been a long period of waiting. There were all those years at school, with the challenge of 'O' levels, then two years later 'A' levels and 'S' levels. Then had come those two years of National Service, far away in Hong Kong. Finally, after demobilisation in March, there had been the months firstly in Paris and then in Madrid where I tried to recapture my French and Spanish languages ready for Year 1.

I arrived in Cambridge and taxied to my Year 1 lodgings with Mrs Kirby, just beyond Parkers Piece, where I found one of my flatmates to be Hassan Quwatly, son of the then Syrian President who would be ousted later by Assad. Then, that afternoon, I finally passed through Great Gate into Trinity College itself.

At last I could settle down. Check where and when were my lectures. Start to have dinners in Hall. Meet and talk with new people. I was in a totally new world, and the last thing on my mind was to read the papers. But then the outside world suddenly started to intrude.

One of those whom I got to know in my first week was an Egyptian freshman, Said Zulfiqar. To start with, we chatted about our courses. But on about the third night of our friendship, he suddenly told me that British bombers had been dropping bombs about half a mile from his home in Cairo. It was the dramatic start of the Suez Crisis.

A short time earlier, Colonel Nasser had nationalised the Suez Canal, and Britain and France reacted with their threat to invade Egypt. Now it was actually happening.

It could almost be said that Said's news largely changed my life, turning me from a person having no interest in politics or world affairs to one who would become committed. Not everyone was as shocked as I was. Britain was still largely a colonial power, and quite a number of fellow students took the simple view that "it served Nasser right". Then again, for many recently demobbed students, thus serving our one year in the Army reserve, the main issue was whether we might be called back into uniform. But many of us did react strongly.

The following morning I found my way into a coffee bar in Petty Cury where quite a number of concerned and angry students had gathered. Our first task was to compose one or two leaflets, and run off many copies. The coffee bar owned a copier, which was a new kind of machine at that time. Our second task was then to distribute the leaflets to every passer-by. I recall that one leaflet urged demobbed students not to respond if called up and urged serving soldiers to refuse to join any expedition to Egypt. This was serious talk, which might possibly have landed us in trouble.

Another very quick result of the attack was the holding of a special debate in the Cambridge Union. I was not yet a member, but joined the many who went along for that debate. The good news was that the Motion, which severely criticised the Government for its action, scored a strong victory.

One further result of the British and French action was that many of us on the following Saturday paid our 10/6 rail ticket to London, and joined the protest march that was due to take place. I remember proceeding as far as we could down Whitehall, waving banners and shouting "Adolf Eden must go!!" Then followed a demonstration in Trafalgar Square at which I heard for the first time that brilliant orator, Nye Bevan and, I believe, Michael Foot also.

Our invasion did not proceed much further or carry on for many days. Clearly it was a political error and, urged by President Eisenhower, the British and French forces withdrew. Moreover there was an unexpected possible consequence. Hungary chose that moment of history to seek its independence from Russian domination. Kruschev, while the eyes of the world were firmly directed towards Suez, cleverly took the opportunity to move in and suppress the rebellion.

For my part, political interest and discussion became a feature of my life and have remained so ever since. It had been a lively introduction.

34   What's in a name?

I am told that I was Colin for the first two or three weeks of my life. But then my mother had her bright idea. She joined the 'G' from her christian name Gladys together with the first three letters of her other christian name Winifred, and created the word 'Gwyn'. And thus it has remained ever since.

To the best of my memory, my first realisation of any possible problem occurred when I was 13 years old and had my first French pen-pal. I was the first to write – a simple letter about my family and where we lived. Then back came his reply. "I am so glad that I have a girl as my pen-friend".

The confusion has lasted on and off ever since that first example. I have no problem at all when people – even the majority – assume that I am Welsh in some way, and that I presumably speak and understand Welsh. This is all very understandable. One needs to be Welsh to really grasp that having the letter 'y' in my name means that I am male and that it would be having an 'e' (i.e. Gwen) that would mean that I was female. Also I have no problem explaining that my name actually means 'white' or even 'pure', in Welsh. In fact I was born almost on the border between Potters Bar (then in Middlesex) and Little Heath. So I am proud to say that I am a cross between a Potters Barbarian and a Little Heathen.

However it sometimes comes as a jolt even now, after all these years, to receive letters that start 'Dear Ms Redgers', or messages asking me to pass on something to my husband. But that has been my life.

Meanwhile I still look back in amusement on that time many years ago, when I was still a student, and became a *'plongeur'* washing up in a Paris restaurant for two or three months. I gained the impression quite soon that the waitresses were rather uneasy about ever having to mention my name. It was not that it was hard to pronounce. Instead it was a question of embarrassment. The problem was that the sound of the word 'Gwyn' in Parisian street dialect has the connotation 'lesbian'. Not surprisingly I changed my French moniker to Jacques, and have kept to that name in Paris ever since.

You may well ask "What's in a name?" After all there are many crimes committed at the font that are vastly worse than the name I bear.

35   The value of memories

Much to my surprise, I suddenly became popular one morning.

I was nearing the end of a recent one-month car trip around Spain and Portugal – partially in new places – partially in places I had known many years ago. That evening I had just booked into a *'hostal'* in Tarragona where I had been a tour rep back in 1958 and 1959 as a student. I mentioned some particular items I remembered to the receptionist, who immediately asked if I would be prepared to meet a friend of his – also in the holiday business – in the morning. I duly agreed.

In fact the friend who I met, Xavi of the firm Itinere, was keen on getting some ideas about how modern tourism in Tarragona – still the only Spanish coastal city that has kept its wonderful beauty and dignity despite the vast-fold increase in tourist numbers – had begun. I was able to tell him that the package holiday movement had really started in 1954 or 1955. Swans Tours advertised "Holidays that you can really afford – £35" and started sending trainloads of people to the Costa Brava which had begun to develop. Couriers and representatives were needed. As a student of Spanish at university at the time, I was available over those summer months. In 1957, I worked in Calella de la Costa and Lloret. Then, in 1958, I was sent to Tarragona where good numbers of Swans tourists had just started to arrive (still by train of course, since air travel to Spain had barely started).

So what was it like? I could tell Xavi the name, Pedro Jornet, of the Director of the Hotel Internacional where I had my office, and also talk about the Astari Hotel down by the beach. Juan Ferre – the tourism chief – became a friend of mine. And so on. Xavi was also interested that I guided groups to bullfights in Barcelona, to the Bolava nightclub, to Poblet and Santas Creus, and once or twice to Montserrat. I took groups also to the Barbera wine distillery and to the Chartreuse distillery, both in Tarragona, and once to the Codorniu distillery further north, where 'Spanish champagne' (now called cava) was produced. I had not however guided tourists within the city itself.

Also within Tarragona, which after all is a provincial capital, were a Poly rep and a Thomas Cook rep, but they tended to have individuals as clients rather than mass tourist parties. Xavi was certainly interested to note that Tarragona's neighbour, Salou, – now a very large resort, with high rise hotels – consisted in those days of not much more than one hotel, a station and allegedly the first campsite in Spain.

I had brought up-to-date a very brief guide for tourists in Tarragona, originally written by a British teacher long resident there, and promised to send Xavi a copy. However what this discussion really brought home to me was that my memories of long ago are not only of value to me (whether to write about, or simply to have), but can also be valuable to others. In this case, they were valuable to someone who was trying to research and write about the start of tourism in Tarragona 60 years ago. That was a meaningful lesson for me to take forward and perhaps think about in other connections.

If any one faculty of our nature may be called more wonderful than the rest, I do think it is memory. There seems something more speakingly incomprehensible in the powers, the failures, the inequalities of memory, than in any other of our intelligences. The memory is sometimes so retentive, so serviceable, so obedient; at others, so bewildered and so weak; and at others again, so tyrannic, so beyond control! We are, to be sure, a miracle every way; but our powers of recollecting and of forgetting do seem peculiarly past finding out.

Jane Austen, Mansfield Park

36   **Climbing**

Much as I enjoyed tree climbing as a child, I never took this on to rock-climbing. In fact the only time I ever tried was at High Rocks, just near Tunbridge Wells, fully roped up.

However mountains, and fell-walking on them, have certainly attracted me all my life. The interest started during a family holiday at Barmouth in North Wales, which was very near to Cader Idris. My father, brother and I started to ascend it, though we never reached the top. Then, from my late teens and every few years until my 40s or 50s, it was the Lake District that chiefly took my attention, either camping on my own, or having a family camping weekend.

Scotland was not far behind. Thanks to the fact that my father was a railwayman, I had enjoyed train travelling in Scotland on several occasions during my school years, and I climbed my first Munro peak just before starting my two years of National Service in the army. Perhaps I have bagged almost a score of Munros in the years that have followed.

So what is it that has always attracted me to sacrificing my comfort zone to struggle up to some cairn on a mountain summit? For me, the special joy comes at that point when you can no longer see the roads and buildings below, and are now in a different world. After that you are left with the challenge of reaching the summit or perhaps a range of summits.

I have certainly enjoyed sharing that pleasure with companions. For example I remember well the occasion when I and my son took advantage of the Shelter Stone on Cairngorm for a night when I was completely exhausted. Would I have managed it on my own, I ask myself? But equally I remember an occasion when it was my dog, Samson, who was the one who was the most exhausted. He had started keenly that day but, far off from the day-to-day life of living in the city, he had tired and his pleading eyes desperately urged me to call it a day and take our uphill walk no further. But then, he was getting old at that time.

My childhood ambition was a simple one. It was to see Mount Everest and hopefully climb it. It was certainly never achieved. But nevertheless I much enjoyed the many occasions when I was able to ascend those small hills that we in Britain call mountains.

37   No longer so fabled

Let me look at this as a 5-stage exercise.

Stage I – 1949

The 1949 book "That Fabled Shore" by author Rose Macaulay is the story of a car journey that she made from the Pyrenees along the whole length of the Spanish shoreline with the Mediterranean and on to the border with Portugal. She reported having seen no other British car during her journey. She made mention of people having a holiday in certain places such as Tarragona or Valencia, and this included some people from abroad. Yet chiefly she concentrated on the description of ancient and quaint towns, beautiful scenery and different ways of life.

Stage II – 1952

I had just started learning Spanish and had enjoyed a two-week course in Spanish run by Professor Allison Peers at San Sebastian. Having about £10 of money left over, I bought a kilometric rail ticket for some £4 which took me on a journey to the more well known places (Madrid, Toledo, Cordoba, Seville, Granada) and finally back as far as Burgos. During this tour, I visited the home of a friend's pen-pal – Isolina – in San Juan de Alicante, just to the north of Alicante itself. She was living in a typical street of about 80 terraced houses, about 100 yards from the sandy beach but with no buildings intervening. We strolled around the village and on the beach, practising each other's language. It was August – the height of summer – and I think that I was the only tourist there.

Stage III – 1957- 1959

The £25 limit on the amount that you could take with you had been removed, and more people were interested in going abroad. A new type of business was formed – the package holiday. Swans Tours advertised "Holidays at prices you can afford – £35". This holiday was to Spain, where the Costa Brava was starting to be developed. The tour company needed three or four representatives in Spain and for me, as a university student studying Spanish, it was an ideal opportunity. Trainloads of several hundred tourists made the journey each week from Britain to the Costa Brava and Barcelona – air flights had barely started. Tossa de Mar was the main venue. In fact a Spanish friend said to me "Just give us Gibraltar, and we will give you Tossa de Mar". A few hotels had recently started business in other places too, such as Lloret, San Feliu and Palafrugell, turning these quiet spots from fishing villages into holiday destinations. The '1000 miles of concrete' were just starting.

Stage IV – 1977

It started as a sightseeing visit to Spain. However we ended up in a hotel within a fairly posh new urbanisation between Murcia and Alicante. This place, Campoamor, consisted of half a dozen tower blocks and perhaps 80 or 90 individual dwellings. It was smart, peaceful and delightful, and we bought a holiday home. Around us were sites where other new urbanisations were starting to be developed. Further to the North were the now-established resorts of the Costa Blanca, plus of course Benidorm. One day my San Juan de Alicante friend, Isolina, took us on a trip to meet her brother's family. I still remember her stating proudly "Look what we Spaniards have achieved!" as we drove past Benidorm – that modern megapolis – on a newly constructed autoroute.

Stage V – 2016

A car tour of Portugal and Spain ended by my driving up the Mediterranean coast of Spain from Gibraltar right to the French border. It was the middle of August – the height of the season – and everywhere teemed with tourists. For me, speaking cynically, it had become like a thousand miles of Blackpool, but with high rises. A totally different way of life had taken over. Yes, Tourist Spain is undoubtedly an achievement of great enterprise. But I also have to say that I am less enamoured of its holiday sites than in the past, and am glad that I am not a "beach" person.

38   **Brexit**

It sounded so unlikely. There had always been Conservative Eurosceptics. John Major had suffered badly from them, famously calling those in his cabinet 'bastards'. Even Margaret Thatcher, in power before him, could not be called a pro-European. Then came the many appearances on television of the beer-drinking Nigel Farage, and the foundation of UKIP. But finally it was the gamble of David Cameron – a prime minister without particular principles but with skill in getting elected – that led to Brexit.

Even when Judy told me that she was going to join UKIP because so many stateless refugees were slipping into her social services area in Kent, I really couldn't believe it. But then, of course, I was a strong supporter of the European Movement. Quite soon the referendum was announced and was carried out completely lawfully. Even the BBC were giving equal time slots to both sides.

For me, it was never an argument. I am European. I like the travel. I adore the cosmopolitan nature of London. I recall that the day we joined Europe when, as a product manager, my Twiglets market expanded from 50 million to 500 million people. I continued to be a strong supporter even though the majority in Europe had clearly misread the euro and its likely outcome, and its effect on the southern Europeans.

And in spite of the fact that the EU never had developed a really good parliamentary system.

But the unthinkable happened. All of the big financial wigs had their say, pointing out the likely negative effects of this kamikaze action – but their words were blown aside as 'scaremongering'. The common sense of voting against something that would make you worse off failed to get through. Instead it was antipathy to Brussels and the wish to 'get our country back' that won the day. It was (horrifyingly) dislike of a multicultural ethnic Britain, and the sheer forcefulness of Boris Johnson and the other 'outers'. The arguments put forward by those who wished to remain seemed boring by comparison, with only Gordon Brown showing any spark.

And thus the ratings for Brexit grew. Yet it was still assumed by the 'powers that be' that somehow it would be 'alright on the night'.

Finally we got to the night. Gibraltar was first to declare. A quite obvious result, but of no significance in the scale of things. But then came a Newcastle result – much worse than expected. And other similar results followed through the night until that final 52% vs 48% vote for Brexit was reached. Those majorities for Brexit spread all across the country (though not in Scotland and London). The 'Remainers' – we in London, those with more years of education, the majority of younger people, most of those in Scotland or Northern Ireland – we could all scarcely believe it.

Naturally there was much talk about reversing the situation, having a second referendum, not accepting a result based on lies and so on. But it was a hopeless case. Gambler Cameron lost his position. A sensible Teresa May would lead us from now on. Although no plans had been made for the future, she would try for the best deal. Still with access to the single market. Still something for the youth. Still the supremacy of the City of London. Hopefully still with free borders. Meeting the wishes of the big firms, of Northern Ireland and Scotland, of investment, of the academic community and so on. Even – and unlikely – meeting the interests of the people of Gibraltar.

And Europe has lost out too. There is now a greater risk of further countries voting to leave. Certainly there is a problem when a union loses one of its strongest members. In fact the position of Europe seems to have weakened in this post-Brexit world.

It is reassuring to know that Britain has 'stood alone' before and has somehow come through it. But it is certainly not very pleasant to be aware that, in the words of the Chinese curse, "we now live in interesting times".

39   Night in a Nunnery

'C'est la vie' should perhaps be called 'Es la vida'. Over the years I have always had a close relationship with Spain. Working there, having a house there, studying there, and certainly visiting most provinces. But perhaps the most remarkable of all was the time I spent a night in a Spanish nunnery.

It all started, back in the 70s, as a normal camping holiday in which I drove with my father as far as Tarragona, and then on to Madrid where he caught a train back to England. It was his first and only time abroad, and was highly enjoyable for both of us. I still had some days to spare, so took the opportunity of driving west to Salamanca, and then on to visit the small town of Alberca which had been apparently unchanged for 200 years. From there I drove up into the largely unknown Hurdes range of hills or mountains where one or two tarmac roads had recently, for the first time, been laid.

It was quite near to the highest part of the road that I was hitch-hiked by a local man, a peasant, who told me that he had been waiting for several hours for a car to come up that road. His request was quite straightforward. His 13-year-old daughter was in a convent, and was going to be received the following morning as a potential novice, so could I help with a lift. The only problems were that his whole family, numbering eight or nine people, wished to attend and that the convent was 30 or 40 miles away on the Extremadura plain at Coria. My Ford estate car was up to the challenge. We bumped happily along the mud track to his village, picked up all the family, and made our way to the Madre de Dios Convent in Coria.

It was my first visit to an enclosed order convent. We arrived in the evening, and made our way to the very old building within the town's walls. There was half an hour of warm communication between the family on one side of the grille, and daughter Marisol and some nuns on the other side. I then received an invitation. Would I be happy to stay the night in the convent, and be present in some kind of sponsor or godparent role at the following day's ceremony? I willingly agreed, and found myself sleeping that evening under the watchful eye of a large Madonna in the visitors' cell within the convent walls.

The following morning saw the ceremony. The family came back from their lodgings, a local priest – male, of course – arrived, and we squeezed into the area just outside the grille. Facing us in their appointed places within the chapel were the Mother Superior, some two dozen nuns, and of course Marisol herself in a gleaming white gown and head dress. The service proceeded with prayers and some chanting, I and two members of the family had to assent to a couple of statements, and 13-year old Marisol was duly received – perhaps for the rest of her life. After that it was a lift back for the family to their mountain village and, for me, a memory that would never go away of a most unusual happening.

Now fast-forward 40 years, in fact to the year 2016 in which I am writing this account.

For the first time for possibly 30 years, I had decided to take my car for a several week tour of Spain and Portugal. I gave myself a wide-ranging itinerary to accomplish. And one element within it clearly had to be 'a must'. Unfortunately I had not kept any record of names and addresses from all that time ago. However I did still have half a dozen photographs of the occasion.

Coria had clearly modernised over the years, but the Madre de Dios convent was still there, just inside the old town walls. As luck would have it, it was the town's feast day. The Sisters were playing their part by selling some convent-produced delicacies, through a floor-to-ceiling grille, to the townsfolk. Visits to the cloisters were now possible. Could Marisol still be in residence, I wondered?

I was able to talk and show the photo of Marisol to three of the nuns, one of whom had been there for 20 years and the other two rather longer. The answer was negative. The two older nuns certainly remembered her well. She had been active and had taken part in a mission to Ecuador. She had a really good singing voice. But in the end she had married a musician and had left the convent. She now lived in Madrid and had a son. Meanwhile her elderly mother had moved to the town of Caceres, in Extramadura.

I passed over my address, and perhaps it did reach Madrid. But there was nothing more to do. At least I now knew what had happened to that sweet girl whom I had met some 40 years previously.

There was one other step to take, so the next morning I drove the 30 or 40 miles to the small villages perched high up in the Hurdes hills. The roads were now all tarmacked and well used. There would be no more waiting for many hours for a car to pass. Unfortunately I could not recognise nor recall the precise village from where the family had come. However I took a stab and entered a bar, where I showed my photos of Marisol and of some family members to the villagers who were there. One of those present claimed to be related, and my heart missed a beat. But then his friends stated that he had been making it up. He was known as a fantasist, and what he had said was untrue. Once again there was nothing more to be done – just a memory to be retained.

Nevertheless, although I was unable to make actual contact with the key people, that nunnery experience of so many years ago remains one of my most treasured memories, and I was glad that I had made the attempt to follow it up.

40   Cycling to Paris

Bicycle travel seems to be making a comeback on Britain's roads. Cycle lanes are now frequent in cities like London, and are often well used. There have always been cycling clubs using the roads at weekends, but road cycling itself would appear to have been largely displaced by cars and even seems a rather risky occupation.

How different from my youth, when roads were largely empty of cars.

My school friend Roy and I were just 15 and had recently become Youth Hostel Association members when we decided to undertake a long cycle ride during the school holidays. It started as the idea of cycling around France but in the end we limited it to cycling to and from Paris. There were of course issues to be faced. Cost was an obvious one, where we would need parental help. Also in Roy's case there was a need for him to obtain a passport. Another issue was whether our bikes were up to standard for the challenge. Mine was an upright Raleigh bike, whilst Roy's was drop handlebar. These issues were successfully solved and we decided to go ahead.

It is interesting, looking back, to note that there were virtually no strong concerns raised by our parents at that time about the idea of two 15-year-old boys cycling on their own to

Paris for a week or two, whether of the risk posed by busy roads or the risk posed by what has now become termed 'stranger danger'.

I still remember setting off from Roy's house, cycling across the Thames and taking the well-named Old Kent Road away from central London. That night we finally arrived and stayed at Canterbury Youth Hostel. The next day we spent some time sitting on the White Cliffs of Dover, and then took the ferry to Calais. Once in France, we worked our way down the coast road to Falaise and then, from Le Havre, we headed along the Seine to Paris.

Our stay in Paris was in the 'Auberge de la Jeunesse' in the 9th arrondissement. It was a popular hostel where we were able to meet hitch-hikers and other travellers from various European countries and also from South America. Several other cyclists were staying there, though none – apart from us – were from England. It was our first time in Paris, and we visited the well-known landmarks. Viewing the Eiffel Tower, seeing the Venus de Milo for the first time, and cycling along the Champs Elysées from the Place de Concorde right up to the Arc de Triomphe and beyond were especially enjoyable.

I must mention one amusing incident which took place near where we were staying just below Montmartre. I was wearing long trousers, but Roy was still in his cycling shorts as we were strolling along when a 'lady of the night' ran over to him and, with an 'Oh là là' of excitement, playfully smacked his bare thighs. It quite made his day!

We stayed in Paris just for three or four days, and then headed back to Calais by a more direct route. By this time, cycling on the right had become automatic. However I still painfully recall those French highways which often stretched for 3 or more kilometres without a bend but possibly with an upward incline. We had to wait until motorways were introduced before such roads became commonplace back in England. In the meantime, our winding roads and fields with hedges were still the order of the day.

In the next few years, I had the good fortune to be able to visit Paris several times, occasionally crossing from Lydd by Silver City Airways, and then hitch-hiking. I even had the experience of washing up as a 'plongeur' in a Champs Elysées restaurant for three months while seeking to improve my French. But I still have strong and most pleasant memories of that first cycling visit.

41 Towards the NHCS?

My purpose in these pages is to give a brief account of what has happened – for me, to me, by me – during my lifetime. Certainly several items concerned with health could be mentioned. For example:

- my hospital stay at the age of seven years when an inexperienced nurse grabbed my broken arm to pull me up the bed, which turned a simple break into a full-blooded fracture.

- the time much later in life when I was receiving a medical. I mentioned to the nurse that I had given up my heavy smoking habit in 1977, and added mischievously that now – almost 40 years later – I was thinking of restarting. Not surprisingly she hit the roof!

- even earlier today, when the doctor's advice to a family member about a small episode of gout was to switch from cider to beer and to cease eating Marmite. (In fairness to the medical profession, I should add that was not the only treatment prescribed!)

However these instances are minor. The really major event which happened in my lifetime was the introduction in

1948 of the National Health Service. It was certainly a major advance on the disorganised range of medical facilities that had preceded it. In future the management of health would be a single enterprise, covering the whole population, and free at the point of delivery. Little wonder that it has become a 'national treasure'.

My own usage of the NHS has fallen mainly into two time periods.

The first was in the years of parenting. Hospital was of course a key factor at the time of childbirth. I remember the fight that I had to be present at the birth of my first-born. I only succeeded when I promised that unwilling Sister in charge that I would leave the delivery ward the moment I felt faint. Then during those years of schooling, nurse consultations and visits to surgeries were necessarily quite frequent, whether for routines such as vaccination or for those mishaps that invariably take place during every child's life. Some items are bound to stand out. Our choice as a GP in those years was Dr Dunwoody, who was the father-in-law of an MP with that same surname. He had a very well deserved reputation as a children's doctor. He also had several ashtrays in his waiting room area, even though his immediate family included another doctor who was the mainstay of ASH – the anti-smoking pressure group.

The other main time period of usage has been (and continues to be) the post-retirement years. When the NHS came into being in 1948, the average male was quite likely to live for only a couple of years or so after his retirement. Now it is more likely to be at least 10, and of course more health conditions arise. In fact we oldies can almost seem to compete over the number of pills that we take. This is of course the time when the NHS truly comes into its own.

I am particularly fortunate in using a local GP surgery which regularly comes right to the top with marks for service in any surveys undertaken. I am also fortunate in having the excellent St Georges Hospital at Tooting as the main one I visit. I am struck by the huge number of services offered and also by the many hundreds of the borough's inhabitants who throng the clinics, wards and corridors every day.

As examples of the care provided, I am the very satisfied recipient of two brand new knees. Would these, I wonder have been freely given and so expertly installed back in those days before the NHS? And another aspect – what on earth would they have cost in the USA? I am always amazed at the fact that a vast number of Americans continue to look down on the provision of health services by the State.

But it is not all smooth – far from it, in fact. As populations live longer and medical treatments become even better, the cost of the NHS escalates. Sadly those who govern us always try desperately to cope by cuts of every kind – of treatments, of personnel, even of availability, rather than by simple taxation rises. I am sure that, if properly explained and presented, we would all pay to keep this national treasure still at its peak.

But at least there seems to be one hopeful movement in opinion if not yet in funding.. This is the increasing realisation that those two costly benefits – Health and Care – must belong together, and that the NHS should, in an ideal world, be re-named the NHCS.

The astonishing fact is that Bevan's vision has stood both the test of time and the test of change unimaginable in his day. At the centre of his vision was a National Health Service, and sixty years on his NHS -- by surviving, growing and adapting to technological and demographic change -- remains at the centre of the life of our nation as a uniquely British creation, and still a uniquely powerful engine of social justice'

Gordon Brown (2008)

42   **Rwanda**

Teaching school students to debate is one thing. But to do this in faraway Rwanda is quite another. However this was the invitation that came my way just a few years ago in 2013.

Rwanda is a country which had experienced a quite horrifying genocide some 19 years before in which the majority Hutu people were urged, including by the nation's radio, to murder the minority Tutsi population. They duly did so, and some 800,000 or more people were murdered.

Much had happened since that time. The country had acquired a stable government, determined to achieve harmony and also to develop the economy. Moreover, although prior to independence it had been a French-speaking Belgian colony, Rwanda had joined the British Commonwealth in 2009. One outcome of this was that it had made the decision to change its second language from French to English, and this had been carried out .

A year prior to our visit, a group of enterprising recent school leavers had taken a further important step. They were determined that Rwanda's future should be decided not by violence but by reasoned argument. To help achieve this in their country, they had therefore established a new organisation – IDebate Rwanda – and were now planning to hold a debate camp in December 2013 for senior school students. Its first week would take place in the Gashora Girls Secondary School, situated on the shore of Lake Kivu, whilst its second week, which would include debating contests, would be held in a school within Rwanda's capital, Kigali.

There was one problem, which was a lack of debating trainers in the country, and IDebate Rwanda therefore turned to Tony Koutsoumbos, founder of Debating London, for help. My own experience lay more in the training of speaking rather than of debating, but nevertheless this was seen as relevant and I was invited by Tony to join him, Jack Watling and an American debater – Jordan Anderson – in a 4-person training team to travel to Rwanda and assist. In addition, we were joined by a filmmaker, Alec Rossiter, whose film of our time out there can be seen on the website www.gwynredgers.com.

It was an amazing experience in so many ways. The training itself was pronounced highly successful, and Rwandan students have since gone on to attend competitive debating events both elsewhere in East Africa and also in the United States. Let me end with some brief points from my own report of the visit.

It was the first time that I had visited the continent, apart from a troopship voyage along the Suez Canal many years previously. At last I could see for myself the richness of the African landscape, as well as the country's considerable poverty. I was also able to fully appreciate the need for the

20-year plan of advancement which Rwanda had set itself. A second key point was to describe and praise highly the spirit, skills and enthusiasm of the 100 or so students who attended the debate camp. This included praising their mastery of the English language which had been attained in that short period of time since English had been adopted as the country's second language.

In addition I outlined a few details of the training which we undertook, including mentioning some of the debate motions themselves. These were largely suggested by the content of the country's 20-year plan, such as for example whether Rwanda might seek to join the union of the other East African states. We visitors had to recognise the very different culture of this foreign country. For example, in a debate on whether or not there should be a rail link to the Congo Republic, which adjoins Rwanda, one unexpected issue which arose and was fully discussed by the participants was 'whether God would approve' of such a step.

This visit was a highly important undertaking for a team from the UK to undertake. I am also extremely glad that, by request, the visit has since been repeated, even though I myself did not participate on that second occasion. Hopefully there will be other such undertakings for Debating London in the future.

43   Those Trinity Years

It's impossible to say much about those all-important university years in just a few words. I found this out myself, and so recently wrote a short book on the subject. (*Those Trinity Years*, available through Amazon or my website). Nevertheless I must try..

My 3 years at Trinity College, Cambridge, not only provided me with a degree, but also with a host of memories. It was a time when less than 5% of British school leavers went on to university, and the bulk of these were from private schools. There were also, however, numerous students from the British colonies (as they then were) and from elsewhere abroad.

Trinity itself was the largest and one of the oldest Cambridge colleges. It had a high reputation as a place of learning which included such eminences as Francis Bacon, Isaac Newton, Jawaharlal Nehru and Bertrand Russell. One of its boasts was to have spawned more Nobel prizewinners than any other British college. In addition, although we were only to learn this later on, it was possibly more responsible than any other college in stimulating Cambridge to be a leading centre for new science-based businesses.

During my time there I had the opportunity to read Modern Languages in Year One, switch to Moral Sciences (viz

Philosophy etc) in Year Two, and switch again to Economics in Year Three. In other words I was able to change, as my main interest changed, from languages to a study of thought, and then on to interest in politics (as this largely is largely determined by economics). Nowadays such switching would be far less possible.

But of course 'education' per se is only part of the mix that you receive from a good university. For some it is a time of major concentration on areas such as science or medicine, or perhaps the academic focus needed for a fellowship. For others it might be the opportunity to spend many hours in developing sporting interests, or perhaps laying the foundations for a sparkling cultural career on TV or stage. My own time and interests included serving on the College Union Committee for two years, starting up and writing a brief but newsy monthly Trinity Bulletin, and running the college's annual Rag Day charity celebration. These activities certainly gave me a wealth of good experience for the years in business that followed.

Also included in my own 'education mix' were numerous other opportunities, such as joining various political or other societies or, on a lighter level, indulging in activities such as punting or even at times night-climbing. Trinity was in fact the cradle of the secret practice of night climbing. The first-ever Handbook, *The Night Climber's Guide to Trinity Roofs*, was written by Geoffrey Winthrop Young (mountaineering pioneer and Trinity graduate) in the 1890s, and interest has continued ever since.

Most of all, my college years gave me the opportunity to meet and develop friendships with a host of fellow students, including some who went on to achieve considerable success and possibly fame in public life. 'Those Trinity Years' were indeed a great privilege for me.

It was at an alumni event a year ago that I was asked "What was it like when you were at Trinity?" It was a question that stimulated me to write of those years, 1956 to 1959. I concluded the book by describing the main differences from the present time, 60 years later. Three of them were the following:

- only 5% of school leavers – mainly from private schools – then attended the few universities which existed. The figure is now nearer 30%.
- Trinity, like most other Oxbridge colleges, was then male only. But of course in most households males were the only breadwinners. How the world has changed!
- All student information came from reading books and listening to lectures. It was quite a number of years before individuals and even many companies would own computers. Mobile telephone, Google search, Wikipedia, social media – all these were in the far-off future.

In appearance, Trinity College may seem like a splendid memorial to the past. But in reality it is living in a quickly changing world.

44 On smoking

My drug of choice was always tobacco. From those first trial puffs at the age of 14 during a school trip to Frankfurt, it was to grow into a serious habit. Obviously it had to be hidden as long as possible from my God-fearing parents. But for me, like for so many, it was a proof of being grown up. Moreover, if you wished, you could even buy your Players Weights singly if money was tight.

Going abroad helped too. Not only was the price significantly less, but it taught me to switch to Gauloise or Gitanes cigarettes (always *sans filtre*) for my 40-a-day habit. It was not surprising that, in one of my later firms, my office should bear the nickname of 'the French brothel'.

Smoking was normal behaviour in life, back in that earlier period. The first action on meeting someone would be to offer or accept a fag. Actors and film stars, both male and female, would be seen smoking. Army life or even civvie life would be interspersed with 'smoke breaks', rather than tea, coffee or comfort breaks. And for those 2 or 3 persons who did not smoke? Tough luck!

However as the years went by, some disturbing factors started to emerge. One of these was the cost, as successive governments realised the huge sums that could be obtained from taxing this near-universal habit. Pockets started to be hurt. Then too, even more seriously, came the first hints that smoking was not beneficial medically. In fact it might even be the reverse.

To cease smoking is the easiest thing I ever did.
I ought to know because I've done it a thousand times.

Mark Twain

I was in my mid-thirties, I recall, when I had my own first doubts. One or two friends had ceased smoking, and perhaps I should too. I knew very little about the difficulty that this would involve. At that time I was applying for a new job, so I decided that I would stop when I left the present firm. It was all planned in my mind. But then those colleagues of mine, whom I would be leaving, generously gave me a marvellous Zippo cigarette lighter as my going-away present. I had no chance!

The next time, a year or two later, was more successful. The medical facts were now pretty certain, and I decided more definitely to stop. It was certainly not easy, but I succeeded – for about six months. But then I was kindly offered a small Hamlet cigar, and that small voice which I thought gone away whispered to me "You've given up cigarettes –not cigars". It took less than a fortnight to find myself smoking eight or nine of those small cigars a day, so I returned to cigarettes as smoking them was cheaper.

But eventually, and possibly inevitably, the time for decision arrived again. It was the end of winter, and unbelievably I had suffered three bouts of bronchitis in the previous eight or nine months. Moreover it was a time of uncertainty and exceptional cost in my life and I was – to put it bluntly – almost broke. The date was 7 February 1977. I rang the office, and pronounced myself ill. Then, until closing time, I passed the day in the local library and spent the evening until bedtime travelling on the Circle Line – all without a cigarette. The next day I repeated the process exactly. On Day 3, I returned to the office – and survived. The deed was done.

I recall those next few weeks being very difficult at times. One reason was that I had lost some of my powers of concentration, and often found myself leafing through trade magazines rather than concentrating on strategy or the job in hand. In my case, it was starting a chewing gum habit that helped me recover my powers of concentration.

Another result of my ceasing smoking, which took me some time to realise, was that I had thereby lost the ability to enjoy an occasional cannabis spliff. This however, in my case, was not particularly important, especially since one of my close friends was highly adept at baking an excellent hash cake.

Now, looking back, I'm glad that I succeeded in giving up smoking. One reason is health. The 'Big C' risk is (hopefully) a thing of the past for me, though unfortunately the 'lung' effect of my smoking years – termed COPD by the medical profession - is present.

However the main reason is the complete change in social customs. We now live in a time when...... smokers must leave their desk and gather in the street ...... perhaps pop outside the house for a moment to have a puff in the garden ...... not light up in a cinema, or on the bus or train, and barely even in their own car. All that must be hell indeed.

However all is not lost. I still hold on to my dying wish, which is to 'go out' smoking an expensive cigar – regardless of hospital rules!

A custom loathsome to the eye, hateful to the nose, harmful to the brain, dangerous to the lungs, and in the black, stinking fume thereof, nearest resembling the horrible Stygian smoke of the pit that is bottomless

James I of England and VI of scotland
A Counterblast to Tobacco (1604)

45 Speakers Club Life

Speaking activity has been my primary hobby for the second half of my life. This is not public speaking to large audiences for profit, nor is it speaking assignments on behalf of a charity or other good cause. Instead it is participating in an organisation devoted to building confidence and speaking skills. I, like the great majority of members, joined in the first place for business advance and self-improvement, but then have continued largely for enjoyment of the activity and the many friendships which have developed.

It all started quite simply. The year was 1980. I had never previously spoken in public, but now had the task in my job of speaking at least once a month to groups of salesmen. My wife drew my attention to a speakers club that had just been established in our town, and I took the plunge. The long story of my time since then – the early years of gaining skills; the years in which I advanced in the organisation; the more recent years in which I spread my wings into other speaking activities such as debating – are recorded in the book ('My Speaking Journey') which I wrote a year ago. However, let me mention some of the aspects.

Firstly, the people. It was long ago established that the normal reason for joining a speakers club was for work purposes – both building confidence and gaining skills. But there are other reasons too. People of school-age sometimes join because they will need these skills, and there is a great dearth in this country's of speaking courses for the young. At the other end of the scale, older people may well join, quite possibly because they enjoyed the activity in their working years and would like to continue. Regardless of the reason for joining, my experience has shown me that almost without exception those who become members are friendly people, sociable in nature and with a variety of interests.

Secondly, a few words about the training which speakers clubs will provide. The basic element is a course concentrating on 10 skills (e.g. structure, voice, use of notes and so on), a Speakers Guide with a very large amount of help, and evaluation of the actual making of all your talks, whether prepared or impromptu. I should also add that speakers club meetings are ideal for learning and practising the skills of chairing meetings, which are so valuable in a person's working life.

Finally there is the range of activities of speakers clubs, which extend well beyond the local club's regular programme. These include conferences and different types of speaking contest both nationally and regionally, which are also highly sociable. Other types of event have taken place over the years such as, for example, the annual selection of a Speaker of the Year, celebrated by a formal Dinner. Those who have been awarded the title and whom I have met over the years include radio and television personalities, leading politicians, a well-known climber and even an Archbishop.

I could go on. For example my interest in speaking gradually widened to include debating, which in many ways is a different skill. Armed with this skill, I have found myself for instance judging school debating contests, becoming a Trustee of a debating organisation, and even having the opportunity of travelling to Rwanda in Africa to help train secondary school pupils in debating.

There are two main speakers club organisations in this country. One is Britain's own Association of Speakers Clubs (ASC), whilst the other is the Toastmasters Organisation founded over 90 years ago in the USA. Both are similar in the way they help. In conclusion, I would recommend joining either one, whichever happens to be the more convenient.

46   Love for languages

I never know why I developed a strong interest in languages, but it has always been there. Perhaps it was because of trying to converse with those Italian prisoners of war whom my father used to invite to our house on a Sunday afternoon. It might even have come from an early visit to Scotland when I had great difficulty in understanding the broad Glasgow dialect and took it for a foreign language.

However the interest was clearly there and, along with an inborn love of travel, has stayed with me for life.

Language study itself began in Year 1 at my grammar school. The language unsurprisingly was French. Year 2 then offered us a choice – Latin or German. I am still surprised that I decided on the unconversational language of Latin, though that knowledge was then in fact a requirement for getting later on into university. Then, in the fifth form, the school offered us the opportunity of an additional language – Spanish – which I immediately grasped.. Hence it was French and Spanish which formed my 'A' levels and which took me on to university.

Meanwhile my foreign travel started with a school trip to Frankfurt, then in the American Zone of Germany, in 1950. It continued strongly with a holiday cycling to Paris and back in 1951 and a train tour around Spain the following year. But then, in 1954, came my two years of National Service.

As someone with 'A' levels in languages, I naturally applied to be one of that small number chosen to study Russian in our service career. I was unsuccessful. However I had the good fortune to be posted to Hong Kong for 1½ years. This appealed greatly to my love of travel but also gave me the informal opportunity to pick up a smattering of Cantonese. Somehow I acquired the name of 'Mr Lo', and could get by for my main everyday needs. However I certainly never learned to read or write Chinese script, and my knowledge of the language has disappeared almost entirely over the years.

Returning to civilian life, I now had six months to try to recover some French and Spanish fluency before my university career started. Spending three months as a 'plongeur', washing up in a restaurant kitchen in the Champs Elysées, certainly helped. This was then followed by a further time in Madrid, attempting to earn a living by teaching one or two students English. Proof that my efforts had worked came from my French tutor at Cambridge. After holding a 10 minute conversation in French with me, he stated that I spoke well, but then added that "It sounded somewhat like kitchen French". Clearly a knowledgeable tutor!

However it was my Spanish that had the most to gain from my university years. I had the good fortune to be a student of Spanish in the years when foreign package tours (travelling by rail, of course) actually began. "Holidays in Spain at a price you can afford – £35", and a revolution had commenced. A new need existed, which was for Spanish-speaking holiday reps. free to be in Spain for the summer. I duly applied, and spent my long vacations for three years in the Costa Brava and Tarragona. It is when you arrive back in England after three months, fall asleep in an English train, and on waking start to speak in Spanish to the English people in the carriage that you realise how your dual language skill has developed!

It is ironic that during my long and varied marketing career I never travelled away from the British Isles on business and never really needed my foreign language knowledge, though of course I was able to retain it somewhat by occasional holidays abroad and talking to European friends here in Britain. In addition I and my wife were the owners for a few years of a small villa in a delightful 'urbanisation' on the Spanish coast south of Alicante.

Interest in languages never goes away. In my case it has possibly even strengthened since retirement.

One reason has been the opportunity to take extended journeys through Europe by car, revisiting favourite areas and seeing new sights, and possibly staying with long-time foreign friends. A second reason, covered more fully elsewhere in these pages, has been my involvement with various incidents in Italy, which led to several longer visits to Genoa and Rome in Italy. There is a third reason too, which developed from joining and taking part in the activities of the U3A (University of the Third Age). This was the decision to study Italian and not rely simply on 'pigeon Spanish' during my visits to Italy.

The old myth states that everyone in the world used to speak a common language. But when they grew too proud and tried to erect a Tower of Babel that would reach right up to heaven, God intervened and confounded their common language. Esperanto and one or two others have tried to plug the gap, but have failed. Thanks to the computer and its USA development, English is becoming a second language to many parts of the world. But meanwhile communication between peoples and hence the study of languages has to be a vital part of our civilisation.

There is only one other answer. That is the Babel Fish used by Arthur Dent in Douglas Adams' *Hitchhiker's Guide to the Galaxy*. By putting a Babel Fish in his ear, Arthur Dent could instantly comprehend anything said to him in any other language.

But that answer may take a long time to come.

47 Music makes the world go round

Of all the noises, I think music is the least disagreeable.
Samuel Johnson

Music may well make the world go round, but it has played a minor rather than a major part in my own life. Nevertheless it has had its moments and therefore needs to be included in these pages. So let me start off by talking about my own playing of instruments.

Having a piano in the house was probably more common in my infancy than it is nowadays. Certainly we had a piano at home, but I cannot recall the family ever singing around it in the evening. I was seven years old when I started my piano lessons with Mrs Jarman, and continued until the age of 14. One of my great pleasures as I progressed was attempting to play traditional jazz. This brings back the memory of a few occasions when, either in his home or my own, I shared some playing with a close primary and secondary school friend, Terry Lightfoot, who went on to lead his own very famous Terry Lightfoot Jazz Band.

I was about 12 or 13 when my interest transferred primarily to the piano accordion or, as it is better known, the squeezebox. My parents very kindly purchased for me a 120-bass Hohner accordion. Most of my playing was totally private though I did on a couple of occasions play this instrument for square dancing amongst that newfangled group – teenagers – in the Youth Fairs which were then starting to be held once or twice a year in my hometown, Potters Bar.

However all that is very much a thing of the past. To this day I still retain my electric piano, though regrettably play it only rarely.

Singing too has been an occasional pleasure, both before and after my voice broke, and at times in a school or chapel choir. My religious background helped, and one of my key memories is being a member of the Billy Graham Choir during that evangelist's famous crusade at Harringay in London. I shall always remember our slow and prayerful singing whilst people from the audience trooped to the front in their search for salvation.

I had a good bass voice in those days, and my special interest was in negro spirituals. In some parts of Britain, especially in Scotland, it is the done thing for each person attending a small party such as a ceilidh to have his or her own 'party piece'. My own would be something like 'Joshua fought the Battle of Jericho', but sadly all that I have left now is a fairly tuneless croak.

For all of us, attending musical events is a great source of pleasure. For me it is less frequent than in the past, but some occasions still stand out vividly in my mind. For example, I recall the first time that I attended an opera. It was Cavalleria Rusticana, and I was almost overcome by the chorus's singing of the Easter Hymn. For me, orchestral concerts could at times be magical, as could some piano concerts which included hearing my friend Sonia Levy playing at the St-Martin-in-the-Fields in Trafalgar Square and the American Tom Lehrer greatly entertaining us once in Cambridge. Being present in a London theatre for early performances of musicals such as *The Boy Friend, My Fair Lady* or *West Side Story* were certainly highlights, and of course I still retain the programmes to remind me.

Music is such a wide field. Let me now move on to the radio, television and recording worlds, especially of popular music. It was in 1952 that the first ever Top 10 of records was started in this country by New Musical Express, with the top place being taken by Al Martino's *Here in My Heart.* Although not an avid follower of pop, one of my strongest memories occurred at a party that we were holding at our home in Fulham in the early 60s. Someone had brought, and put on the turntable, a disk featuring an unknown singing group, and all present stopped dancing just to listen. The artistes had an unusual name. They called themselves 'The Beatles'.

Quite recently, the musical world celebrated the 50th anniversary of the concert held in Hyde Park by the Rolling Stones. This particularly interested me, since I was sitting happily on the grass for that original concert. Then too I have the memory of those quite frequent late night occasions when Dudley Moore, having performed in some heatre professionally that evening, used to pop into the Establishment Club in London's Old Compton Street, and entertain us on the piano for a further hour or so.

Nowadays music continues to dominate the airwaves and is warmly appreciated by worldwide armies of fans. For myself, however, I confess that I remain an unreconstructed 'Abba-ist' in my taste, just occasionally foraying into listening in awe to some new and highly appealing artistes such as Canada's K.D.Lang or France's Zazzy. And even though not at all involved myself, I have to agree that music still makes the world go round.

48   The Dunmow Flitch

Something in me enjoys old customs. I like the fact that clog dancing still exists, and also the fact that the Doggett Coat and Badge Race still takes place each year on the Thames. I gained great pleasure from living near enough to visit the annual Cheese Rolling event in the Cotswolds from time to time. Perhaps too the description 'old customs' may even apply to popular events such as test matches, the University Boat Race or the Cup Final, since each of these date back to Victorian times. So when my daughter told me that she was planning to live in Great Dunmow in Essex, I was immediately thrilled. The reason of course was that Great Dunmow is the home of the Dunmow Flitch annual trial. It was mentioned in the 1362 book *The Vision of Piers Plowman*, and also by Chaucer in *The Wife of Bath's Tale*, and still I believe the only event of its kind in the world.

The 'flitch' itself is a long leg of pork or bacon, gifted by a local butcher for the purpose, whilst the trial – impossible as it sounds – is of married couples, to decide whether or not they have had dissension of any kind during the last year. Those who can prove that their marriage is indeed blissful are awarded a flitch.

Nowadays the event is held every four years and I was able to be present at the most recent. The event was well-publicised locally, a flitch was very much on display, and a large marquee was erected for the trial.

The main speaking participants were duly appointed. These were the judge, counsels for prosecution and defence, the court usher and of course the jury which consisted of six local maidens and six local males. In addition there was the supporting cast. Some instrumentalists – almost a village band – performed on the journeys to and from the 'courthouse' marquee. Additionally a body of local men, suitably attired in old farmworking smocks, were present, primarily to carry in triumph any client couples who passed the test. And finally there were the defendants themselves – five brave married couples prepared to face up to questioning about their marital happiness in a series of separate trials

The trial which I attended lived up well to my expectations. 200 people or so were seated in the marquee, which I should perhaps call the public gallery. Orders were barked out to us – "All rise", and so on – and we meekly obeyed. Then the cast assembled and the cross examinations began. The two Counsels certainly played their part well with much wit. Instances such as "I didn't tell her what I was buying" (i.e. for her birthday) were skilfully transposed by the prosecution into an act of 'non-communication' rather than as one of happy surprise, and there were many similar examples to enjoy. Finally the jury retired and returned quite soon after with a verdict.

This year, three couples were awarded a flitch and two returned home flitch-less. Those who had succeeded were carried, seated in their specially carved chair and accompanied by music, on the shoulders of the bearers to the town square where further celebration took place. Their year of marital bliss had been proved. Or – as a cynic might say – they could now argue without risk of losing the bacon.

It had been a great day – a unique leftover from Olde England – and long may this ancient custom continue. But who can know the future? Maybe a future generation could one day change the award from a bacon flitch to a meat more acceptable to some faiths, or even to a non-meat more acceptable to the growing vegan community.

49   The U3A and Lifelong Learning

Older and retired people are sometimes heard to complain that "I'm bored. There's nothing to do". For my part, the opposite is the case, and one of the chief reasons is the remarkable University of the Third Age, most commonly known as the U3A. First appearing in France back in the 70s, it surfaced in the UK in a rather more popular and less academic way in 1980. Since then it has grown at a remarkable rate to the figure of some 1000 branches and some 400,000 or so members. In terms of structure, it has a head office in Bromley. However each of its branches is an independent Trust in its own right.

People stumble across it in various ways. My first experience of the U3A was its Canterbury branch which my weekend partner of many years, Judy, was persuaded to chair for three years. I was certainly impressed by the body, and in due course joined my own local Merton U3A branch.

The choice of activities open to me was wide. Should I join a music group, or study computing, or perhaps family history? Or what about activities that were more social in character, such as walking, table tennis, or even Scrabble? I quickly settled for two. One was a group meeting fortnightly that discussed Current Affairs, which had long been an interest of mine. The other was an Italian conversation group, which would prove particularly useful as I was then needing for other reasons to learn and converse in that language. These, plus my local branch's monthly talk and occasional coffee mornings, were a start.

The core philosophy of the University of the Third Age is that a member should seek to give as well as to take. I soon realised that I was in a position to be able to "give" instruction and leadership in the areas of speaking and debating. I therefore established a new group to hold fortnightly speaking and debating meetings, which I and (hopefully) the group's members have now enjoyed for six years. Other U3A opportunities also presented themselves. For instance I found myself in a team assisting the Post Office Museum research the subject of 'sport on stamps', and also leading an eight-session course discussing the (non-existent) United Kingdom constitution.

One of the three far-sighted innovators who established the U3A in this country, Peter Laslett, was a Fellow of my Cambridge college, Trinity. During my residence there. I walked past him most days, but did not know his area of study. Now I know it and am both grateful and impressed. Certainly there is absolutely no need for any older or retired person ever to say again "I am bored".

50 The good ship 'Devonshire'

1954 to 1956 were my National Service years. By October 1954, I had survived my initial weeks of square bashing, or obedience training as it should be called. I then had two months of radar training in Tonfanau Camp on the coast of Wales, and also a further two months of surveyor training on Salisbury Plain. Finally I had received my posting and was naturally very pleased that it would be in Hong Kong. Then had come a brief leave and some fresh kit for a hotter climate, and it was now time to set sail.

I embarked on the troopship HMS Devonshire moored on the Mersey in Liverpool, and found to my surprise that my cousin Peter was also on board, heading towards Singapore. The journey would take some three weeks, and we quickly got used to the daily routines and drills. The first hurdle was to cross the Bay of Biscay, always known for its heavy seas. Sadly quite a number of us succumbed to a bout of seasickness. But then quite soon came that view of Gibraltar and a fine weather cruise along the length of the Mediterranean to Egypt and the Suez Canal. It was while we were moored in Port Said at the start of the canal that a most amusing experience happened.

On arrival, we had all gathered on the deck to observe the lively harbour life. This consisted mainly of numerous bumboats whose occupants' sole purpose was to sell us their wares. Finally we were ordered to return below and pay no further attention. Being keen to enjoy the view further, and although viewing had been prohibited, I perched myself upon a toilet and continued watching the lively scene through a porthole. It was then that, to my consternation, two armed Egyptian soldiers entered and called out to me. I could spell trouble. Nevertheless I stood to attention before them, addressed them as 'Sir', and waited for what they would say. However they said nothing. Instead, to my great relief, one of them rolled up his sleeves to show a gleaming array of watches for sale.

Finally the Devonshire cast off and made its way via the Suez Canal and the Red Sea to its next stop, Aden, where we could at last go on land for a few hours. The area where we stepped ashore was also full of noisy vendors, though they had little chance of selling much to a shipload of conscripts whose pay in those days was a meagre four shillings per day. But once on dry land, it was a real delight to be able to wander through Aden's streets and discover people living such a different way of life from ours.

It was fairly similar in Colombo, capital of the country Sri Lanka which back in those colonial days was called Ceylon. Once again it was a chance to explore a new culture. I certainly enjoyed the experience, and my day there included both a long rickshaw ride and – to my great surprise – the opportunity to watch a snake charmer carry out his trade.

Our journey continued. Next came Singapore and once again the opportunity to spend several hours exploring that famous outpost of Empire. Cousin Peter left the Devonshire at that point and was transported with his colleagues to the Changi RAF base where he would be spending his next year. I, meanwhile, was able to see other landmarks of Singapore, such as the well-known Raffles Hotel. There was however one drawback which rather spoiled the day (or should I say 'which put a damper on things'?). That was the fact that on that particular day the city recorded a rainfall of about 11.5 inches, which was very near its record.

It was also perhaps a sign of the weather to come as we proceeded up the South China Sea. Unfortunately we were following closely behind a typhoon and the sea was certainly turbulent. A large unit of Gurkha soldiers who had joined the ship at Singapore suffered badly. It was not at all surprising that only a few of them appeared for breakfast or lunch.

Finally, after our long journey through many time zones, Hong Kong came into sight, firstly the island and then the mainland. At last we could shoulder our kit bags and march off to our new life.

In conclusion, let me say that my time on the good ship HMS Devonshire has been the only cruise of my life. I may have been squeezed into cramped quarters, with no modern comforts, and certainly not wearing suitable sunbathing clothes, but that trip remains one of my most cherished memories.

51   Four-legged friends

It would be hard to write these pages of *C'est la vie* without some reference to Bloggs, Samson and Mabel. Maybe they differed from me by having four legs rather than two, but they shared several years of the life of which I am writing.

None of them was my first pet. The animal which I regarded as our pet during my childhood was Talkie. The name suggests an animal which communicates well, perhaps even a parrot, but the opposite was the case. Talkie was in fact a tortoise of indeterminate age who shared our garden both before and during those years. He would sleep through the winter in his own preferred accommodation, hidden almost within our greenhouse. But then, each Spring, he would reappear, spend hours parading on our back lawn and flower beds, and was totally happy to be in the presence of humans.

So could Talkie be called a pet? I'm not sure. We normally think of a pet as something to stroke or possibly play with, and there were to be none like that until I was married and had children in my household. Then came the three that still stand out most strongly in my mind.

The first of these was Bloggs, or 'Mr Bloggs' as he was often called, who was a terrier-like mongrel. He first came into our life as a very welcome daily visitor to the weekend 2-up 2-down cottage which I rented for some time in the village of Ringstead in the Northamptonshire countryside. The children were very pleased when he joined us in our London home. He proved a lively addition, always responsive to children and adults alike. His daily walks tended to be exploring Shepherds Bush Green, and he lived a largely trouble-free life. There was however one day when the opposite was the case and he nearly came to an early end.

The occasion was a camping weekend in the Lake District. For Bloggs, this was a time when he could run free without a lead and make friends with other campers. But one morning came a visit from a farmer bearing a shot gun. It emerged that our happy-go-lucky pet dog had found a new pastime of which we were unaware – namely the chasing of sheep. This could of course be a capital offence for a dog, unless it was a border collie. Fortunately Bloggs had quite soon given up the sport and had returned to our tent, but it had been a close shave. He visited the Lake District again, but was always kept on the lead.

The next dog I should mention was Samson, who arrived as a puppy a few years later. He was a white labrador of pedigree stock. Compared with Bloggs, he was more tranquil and easily trained. It was rare that he needed to be on a lead, even in busy streets. A brief command completely sufficed.

There came the time when I was courting Julie. Samson would share my weekend visits, and proved highly popular with her children. Then, when we bought our house in

Cheltenham, Samson readily adjusted. He much enjoyed life, especially the occasional Cotswold walks, and certainly never gave the many sheep that he met any trouble. But of course all pet owners have to face up eventually to the fact that the life span of a cat or dog is only a fraction of their own and may well be shortened by illness. Thus Samson, as Bloggs before him, eventually became just a happy memory for us all.

And so to the third canine friend. This was a springer spaniel who bore the name Mabel. She too was of pedigree stock, though with a 'droopy eye' condition that would prevent her from being shown. Constantly playful, she was very much a home-loving pet. We all still remember the Christmas occasion when our cats cleverly knocked the plate of freshly cooked roast turkey from the top of the fridge onto the kitchen floor, whereupon Mabel carried it off via the dog flap to her own private picnic in the garden with only cats for company.

Over time, I have also been privileged to share a house with quite a number of cats. There were Buster, Freaky, Fergie and others too. I remember them fondly, but times change. Pet ownership for me is a thing of the past. Nowadays my lifestyle and my place of residence mean that I have to manage with the pigeons and occasional squirrels that appear on the balcony. But the earlier memories die hard.

52 Family history up to date

ooking back into a family's history is always fascinating. From which bishops or criminals, landowners or serving maids did you spring two, three, or four centuries ago? My brother Brian became interested in this and traced the family line of the Redgers name back to about 1700. But, for a change, instead of looking back, why not scan sidewards and take a look at the more recent generations?

Let me begin with a brief look back, starting with my father's side. Born in Paddington with a policeman as his father, his family then moved from Paddington to Potters Bar. In due course the six children were married and some entered the job market. Auntie Lily for example was one who had a career and only married later in life. She entered the nursing field and became an assistant matron in a Barnet hospital. Then, during the war from 1939 to 1945, she joined QARANC, the Queen Alexandra's Royal Nursing Corps. She served in a deputy matron capacity firstly in Nigeria, then on a troopship and in Burma, and finally in a field hospital in Austria at the end of the war. She then became a district nurse based in Shenley in Hertfordshire. Another sister who entered the job market was Auntie Grace. She was a conductress on the buses during and after the war, when her husband, Dennis, came back from army service and joined her as the bus driver. Later on they became landlords of a well-patronised public house near Hatfield where she acquired the soubriquet "the Duchess", carrying on as landlady into her 80s. Grace, like her sister Phyllis, was long-living, and both passed 100 before they died.

My father's only brother, Uncle Don, worked within the radio industry servicing transmitting stations, while my father had a railway career from the age of 14 to 65, firstly as a signalman and then as an inspector where he became widely known as Teapot Charlie. Due to his religious beliefs, he was a conscientious objector during the war years, but nevertheless was awarded the BEM (British Empire Medal) for particularly notable service during that time. This was naturally a source of great pride to our family.

Switching to my mother's side, her 'absenting' father had been a salesman for Singer sewing machines. On her own mother's death, she became a ward of 'Grandpa Barham' who was a Southampton Docks employee. Interestingly his family claimed one of the Tolpuddle Martyrs as their ancestor. Meanwhile my mother's sister (my Auntie Dorothy) went to London to work in the Dickens & Jones department store, and was married to my blind Uncle John.

That was the generation immediately before me. I now move to my generation. Dot and John had no children, my parents had my brother and me, and my father's brothers and sisters produced between them a total of seven who were therefore my cousins. Some of these had (or have had) interesting life experiences. For example one lives in Paris with a small holiday home in the Riviera in the summer, whilst another lived for a few years in Italy but is now happily married and living in Florida.

To complete the picture, I go to the next generation. My brother and several of my cousins of course married and produced children, as did I. In my case it is slightly more complicated since I married twice. Through my first wife Dickie, whose parents had both a Scottish and Argentinian background, I have two children and a grandchild. Then, through later marrying Julie for close on 20 years, I acquired five stepchildren, we (informally) adopted Claudia, and my own two children each acquired five stepbrothers or stepsisters.

I leave you with a final thought about family history. Genealogy nowadays is largely a question of going back to the early church records and various birth and marriage certificates, whilst the advent of computerised records greatly simplifies such studies. But social conditions change. For example, whereas less than 5% of births in London in the 50s were from outside marriage, 47% in 2012 came from outside marriage. The fact that there is a decline in marriage and an increase in divorce played a part in this, and will certainly make life more difficult for would-be family historians in the future. Could it be that DNA records might one day become a main tool?

53   The place of Religion

These pages attempt to briefly touch on the important episodes of life. What could – for some people – be more important than religion? So this has to be included and here is my story.

My brother and I were brought up in a Plymouth Brethren household. This is a particularly extreme branch of religion both in behaviour and belief. From a behavioural point of view, the attempt is made to follow the edict "Do not yoke yourself with non-believers". Thus close friendships tended to be within the faith. Moreover restrictions such as keeping out of cinemas and closely observing Sundays were quite strictly kept.

As an evangelical church, the core of the faith was the need for conversion, thereby achieving salvation and everlasting life. This comes about not by good works, but by repentance and belief that Jesus died for our sins. And so, at about the age of 12, I found myself repenting and accepting Jesus as saviour, and was duly baptised.

To a greater or lesser extent, my belief continued for another 10 years or so, though I was probably more a sinner than a saint in behavioural terms. During my secondary school days, for instance, I always 'broke bread' on a Sunday morning and was a member of Billy Graham's choir in his

Harringay crusade. Then, during my National Service in Hong Kong, I was a very loyal church attender, including mixing frequently with some of the numerous missionaries forced to flee China when the communists took over. Incidentally one of these was Gladys Aylward who was portrayed in the film 'Inn of the Sixth Happiness'. Indeed for a time I even considered becoming a missionary or a minister, though I soon set that idea aside.

So what happened? All that I can say is that on my return home and from the start of my university life, my religious views and practices rapidly changed. Although still fascinated by theology – comparative religion and practices such as mysticism have been a lifelong interest – I ceased to attend a church.

Not surprisingly there have been a few times when I found myself attending church services. The years of my second marriage are an example. Julie had been a loyal member of her church choir when younger, and has maintained much of her faith (including ministry team membership) up to the present day. But I found it much harder myself having to sing hymns and share in prayers in which I certainly did not believe.

But one thing that life has taught me is that the unexpected can often happen. Now, after all those years of non-attendance, I have become a regular Sunday morning attender at a church. There is, however, a difference. It is a Unitarian Church, which thereby caters for people of no faith as well as for those having a faith. It happened quite simply. A friendship, which developed with that church's minister in a debating club which we both attended, led to my attending his church and finding it a pleasant experience.

I have never had any wish to persuade others to give up their faith. Indeed I have nothing but approval for those who pray to their God and help sustain their places of worship. It is simply that I felt hypocritical in pretending the same. But now, with our congregation which mixes Christian believers with Buddhists, agnostics and atheists I am wholly comfortable. My own attendance is nothing at all to do with worship. Instead it is a time to fully appreciate all those other aspects of religion such as time to reflect and remember; the reality of spirituality; a community based on friendship; and the help given to others less fortunate.

And, of course, once again I am enjoying a Sunday activity as I did long, long ago.

54 Money marketing

t was in 1971 that I switched from product marketing (biscuits) to money marketing (unit trusts), and became only the seventh marketing person in the City. The MD was Charles Wodehouse, previously Marketing Director of Golden Wonder, who had been the sixth. The company, Hill Samuel Unit Trusts, was a subsidiary of a leading merchant bank. Not only was the discipline of marketing new, but also – almost uniquely – the company had just broken new ground by relocating from the City, though only by a dozen miles to Croydon in the suburbs.

t was a fascinating time to be there since even the basic aspects of 'marketing', such as marketing PR, marketing planning, and even investment advertising and product costing were new to financial services. There were no guidebooks, and these practices – common in the consumer field – had to be developed by us from scratch. A separate innovation just starting to appear in the financial services industry was sports sponsorship. In fact we were approached by an ex-army friend of mine, Bruce Tulloh, who had gained fame by running right across the USA, to sponsor a marathon in the Newcastle area. This would have been the forerunner of the very successful Great North Run and indeed of the later London Marathon. I often regret that the company decided to decline that offering.

Sales were growing strongly but then, as can happen in any financial services business, the company itself was forced to shrink due to a severe market crash. I was by then Marketing Director, but was transferred from the marchant bank's unit trust subsidiary to run the marketing in Hill Samuel Life, its life insurance subsidiary. It was an opportunity to get to know the lively field of life assurance and – more importantly – to get to know the Sales Director's assistant, Julie.

Three years later saw a further major change. This was an invitation from my earlier boss, Charles Wodehouse, to join him as Head of Marketing in Trident Life in Gloucester. That is how, in November 1977, I came to have a new house, a new wife, a new job and a new department in the Cotswolds. Once again this was a most enjoyable role which combined both market planning and marketing support.

A special feature of Trident Life was the company's lively PR and marketing support programme which fell primarily into my lap. Externally we set out to be extremely prominent in the annual Life Assurance Congress in Wembley. This was because recruiting more self-employed salesman was a key company aim. Not only did we have a stand in the Congress, but we also made ourselves more visible by linking in some way with special visitors such as Keith Castle, the first person to have received a heart transplant. Another was Janet Brown who was the first comedy star to impersonate Margaret Thatcher. All who were at the final meeting of one Congress will recall standing to applaud her arrival on stage ("Please welcome our very special guest who, because of the importance of the life insurance industry, has come here directly from Chequers to be with us today") and – a few minutes later – the realisation that they had been hoaxed.

Meanwhile back in our home area, our Chairman invited Prince Charles to come over from Highgrove as a visitor to an orchestral concert we arranged and sponsored in Gloucester Cathedral, and – much less formally – Princess Anne's then husband, Captain Mark Phillips, agreed to be our guest at a celebration fair held in Cheltenham. The company was also the sponsor of the Tour of the Cotswolds cycle race, and every year we sponsored Gloucester Swimming Championships where I became at times the announcer and was fortunately able to spend time with international swimmers such as Duncan Goodhew.

So why, I have been asked, did you decide after four or five years to leave Trident Life? A simple answer. The company was taken over – a frequent happening in the financial services industry at that time – and I found myself downgraded from No. 1 in marketing to No. 3. I had had an excellent time at Trident Life, but it was on to pastures new – and these were back in the City of London.

55   Being a Londoner

We are all happy and proud of our home city or place of birth (or should be). But I still think that London is special and – as the song puts it – "I get a funny feeling inside of me, just walking up and down". It's difficult, but I'll try to summarise why in just a few quick paragraphs.

First, the sightseeing. Where else could you find an Abbey, two cathedrals and numerous Wren churches; a Tower, plus Parliamentary and Royal palaces; imposing monuments; a large theatre land; so many museums; and – nowadays – Canary Wharf and the Shard?

Still on the subject of sightseeing, London has its magnificent River Thames flowing from its estuary down to Richmond and Kingston under an array of splendid bridges. I was fortunate enough to be a Day 1 visitor to the so-called 'Wobbly Bridge' joining the Tate Modern to the City. I still feel sad that the 'wobble' was corrected, and we thereby lost what would have been a rival to Pisa's leaning tower.

London is a hot-bed of history from Roman times to the present day. It has for instance been the site of a Royal execution, massive protest marches and the world's first underground railway. Great commemorations continue to be held, whether they are in honour of a new Lord Mayor of the City, or Coronations, royal weddings and even memorable State funerals. In my younger years, London suffered the Blitz, but overcame it to put on the Festival of London in 1951. More recently in 2012, London staged (for the third time!) the Olympic Games.

Then there are the excellent residential areas. London's 'villages', such as Highgate, Hampstead, Dulwich and my own Southfields. And more expensive areas such as Mayfair, Kensington, Chelsea, Fulham and nowadays even parts of East London.

Most important of all, London is the home of Londoners, whether Cockney or other English ancestry, or arriving from elsewhere. From earlier groups such as the Jewish refugees of the last century, we have moved to the Caribbean communities of Brixton and Notting Hill, the Indian and Pakistani communities of both the East End and of Ealing and Southall in the West, the many immigrants from the white Commonwealth, and nowadays the large number of new friends from the European Union. We are perhaps the leading Cosmopolitan city of the world, and it certainly makes me proud to be part of it.

Two years ago, in a debate, my son Adrian was the proposer of the Motion '*that London should be independent*'. The Motion was carried. It was intended humorously, but should it possibly now be our aim after the Brexit idiocy?

56   Days of protest

I was asked a few days ago whether I would come along and join other people in a 'lying down' protest in a Heathrow terminal. My answer was "No". It was not a cause that much interested me and, in any case, I protest only rarely. But I have been involved in protests from time to time, and here is the story.

My first ever protest took place just a week or two after I started my three years at Cambridge. The Suez Crisis erupted, and I joined a small group printing pamphlets denouncing Britain's air attacks and the planned invasion of Egypt. In addition I was one of many hundreds who marched down Whitehall shouting "Adolf Eden must go!!" and then assembled in a rally in Trafalgar Square to hear such speakers as Aneurin Bevan. Incidentally my only other protest action as an undergraduate was to take part in an 'Anti-Ugly' march shouting abuse at a new building within Downing College.

The 60s were the years of CND (Campaign for Nuclear Disarmament), in particular the annual Aldermaston march. I was not a supporter, mainly on the grounds that I felt it impossible to uninvent something that had been invented. In any case I still feel it likely that it was the balance of nuclear power that largely prevented we Europeans from having our regular wars with each other in the years after 1945.

Nevertheless I would attend CND's and the Committee of 100's Trafalgar Square rallies on occasions. It was many years later that a very close debating and speaking friend, Mike Douse, told me that he had been an assistant to Bertrand Russell in those Committee of 100 years, and I must therefore have seen him being lifted by police from the famous sit-down in the Parliament Square roadway and – together with his boss and others – being transported to a day or two's full bed-and-board in Brixton Prison.

Grosvenor Square was another site for occasional near-violent protests, where I very much appreciated the spoken attacks on the Vietnam War delivered by Tariq Ali and others. It was my introduction to close contact with the galloping horses of the Metropolitan police. I also recall a totally different protest one evening outside the Chinese Embassy in Upper Regent Street. Unusually it was not staged by any of the normal left-wing groupings but by a fairly small and polite group from the centre and the right of the political spectrum. The reason I remember it particularly was for the thoughtful discussion that took place to decide whether it was lawful and not too rude to shout any slogans, and the lack of passion when they finally voiced some.

After the Millennium, I started to meet more protesters. By that time I had joined the Cogers –a debating society whose members extended from a few from the far-right to some anarchists and others from the far left. Free speech was and remains the ethos of the Cogers. The society was particularly proud of the fact that, at the start of the war, its members politely applauded a strongly pro-Hitler speech delivered by one of its BUF (British Union of Fascists) members, who shortly afterwards was arrested under the Defence Regulation 18B and kept in custody for the remainder of the war.

It was at the Cogers that I met Mark Covell, a journalist who had been beaten into a coma by the Genoa police in their infamous night-time raid on a G8 protesters' dormitory. 57 victims were hospitalised on that occasion. We became close friends, and I was able to assist him in a small way to eventually gain very sizeable compensation.

Mark's main work was for the British branch of the worldwide Indymedia, global independent publishing network, which can be described as the protestors' main voice. My first visit with him was to Edinburgh to attend some of the events of the Anti-G8 protests held in 2005, and also to chair a London rally of the European Social Forum. The event was held in London's Conway Hall, and my speakers included the first talk ever to be given by one of the three so-called English 'terrorists' just released from Guantánamo Bay.

Later on, Mark's main interest became climate change, which was a cause dear to my own heart too. For instance, I accompanied him to meetings with politicians both in Brussels and in Rome, as well as nearer home, and additionally was a visitor (as opposed to a full camper) to the Climate Camps held at Kingsnorth in Kent and on Blackheath in London. This gave me first-hand experience of the police overreaction that totally legal protesters quite often face. For example I was thoroughly searched under 'terrorism legislation' before I could enter the Kingsnorth Climate camp, and was pleased to accept a £300 compensation cheque from Kent's Chief of Police once his force accepted, belatedly, that we climate change protesters were not in fact terrorists.

So what protest will come next? I certainly do not intend to protest outside the Russian Embassy, as recently – and very surprisingly – recommended by Boris Johnson. In any case other methods of assisting campaigns now exist. For example Parliament now has a department and useful procedures for dealing with Petitions, including the recent one which sought to ban Donald Trump from entering Britain. Crowd-funding and campaigning organisations such as Avaaz also exist and are often achieving good results.

I think my days of protesting (and of being kettled) are likely to be over, but I remain proud of the great British traditions of protest and free speech.

57   Pleasure in writing

Writing is a new hobby which I began just two or three years ago. It is proving enjoyable for the author and hopefully quite interesting for the reader too. Here is the background.

Writing, like reading, comes early in life. The simple 'thank you' letters that we had to send before social media took over were the start. They then graduated on to those scores of essays that we had to compose in school and university. Careers differ. However mine certainly included numerous reports over the years, often quite lengthy, whilst my marketing responsibilities also necessitated a great deal of copywriting and brochure preparation. I even had a dream that, if I were to lose my job, I might earn my living as a travel writer. But the question of writing for pleasure or even for profit in other ways never crossed my mind. Life was too full and busy. Then, in my late 70s, two reasons for writing occurred.

One of these was travel. In 2013, I indulged myself by embarking on a 5-week driving tour covering a dozen European countries. My primary purpose was to meet again friends on my Christmas Card list whom in some cases I had not seen for 30 or even more years, whilst my secondary purpose was to visit again numerous places that had charmed me. Say the word 'Venice', and you will understand what I mean. That trip clearly needed writing up and posting on a personal website for others to read. Also in that same year, I was invited to join a small team training some school pupils in Rwanda in the techniques of debating. To me it was a marvellous adventure in a part of the world which I had never visited. That too needed a brief report on the website, which I therefore wrote.

The second reason for starting writing was more memoir-based. Like so many other senior citizens, I had enjoyed an interesting life and was now surrounded by drawerfuls of paper and other memorabilia. Should one attempt to pass any of this on, or never mention it and simply leave it to be discarded by one's heirs? I decided on the former and, to my surprise, found the act of composition most enjoyable.

It was another hobby that prompted my first writing of this kind. That was my involvement with speakers clubs and later on with debating. It was 35 years since I had stumbled unknowingly into a newly-formed speakers club in Cheltenham, where I then lived. In the years that followed I made many good friends, I learnt and taught public speaking, I started new clubs and achieved high office, and I planned and hosted many events. In addition I discovered the joys and stimulus of debating, which also led to numerous memberships and experiences. I had retained many records and it therefore became both pleasurable and possible to write and publish *My Speaking Journey*.

That was Book No. 1, and Book No. 2 soon followed. The trigger was an event at my old Cambridge college where an alumni officer, some three or four decades younger than me, asked "What was it like here in your time?" That for me was an obvious invitation to write the story, and hence "Those Trinity Years" was created and published. Now, as you can see, the bug has bitten more deeply and you are reading the result.

My own technique in writing is a scribbled draft summary, followed by composition using voice recognition software. Then follow the editing and correction stages. Publishing was a total new world for me, and I was fortunate to find a highly competent small firm whom I could work with most happily. But what about the question of selling?

As I said at the beginning of this series of episodes of my life, "Writing is a new hobby which I started just two or three years ago. It is proving enjoyable for the author and hopefully quite interesting for the reader too." In other words, I am fortunate that selling is in no way the main purpose of my writing, though it obviously helps if some of the cost is covered. It is the creation – the opportunity to share the incidents of my own life with others – which is the purpose of my own writing, and I recommend the composing of memoirs as a hobby to others.

58 Back to Blighty

Soldiers the world over are prone to lie on their bunks and tick off the days until their tour of duty will end. I was one of them. My calendar had a note of that day when my two years of National Service would end and I would return to civilian life. It had a note too of that day, some 4 weeks earlier than my demob day, when I would be leaving Hong Kong.

Finally that day arrived. Totally packed, those who were leaving took their flight from Kai Tak airport bound for Singapore where we would be spending three days. I had one great surprise while I was there. A pair of hands clapped over my eyes as I sat by the NAAFI club's swimming pool. They belonged to my school classmate John Brown who was serving with the RAF. One other memory of those final three February days in Singapore was that the temperature was still over 90° (fahrenheit) just before midnight.

Our flight back to England was to be in a fairly small Hercules (I believe) aircraft, and there would be four or five stops. The first of these was Bangkok. Unfortunately we were able to stretch our legs for only half an hour before resuming, but I retain a strong memory of seeing two splendid Buddhist temples quite near to the airport. Then came Karachi. There we were taken by bus to spend the night in a small hotel in the outskirts. Sadly we were not allowed to leave the hotel, and I have no special memory of Karachi.

It was a similar routine at Bahrain, our next port of call. Some two hours to stretch our legs, and we were again on our way. The view through the plane's window of those mountains and sandy areas before we reached Bahrain, and that flight across the Saudi Arabian desert which followed it, still come vividly to mind. I also recall years later the words of the Iranian girlfriend of a stepson. She was living in England but really wanted to go back to Iran on the grounds that "England is so green!"

Finally our plane reached the Mediterranean and accomplished its short flight to Nicosia airport in Cyprus. It was a time of great unrest in that British colony as Colonel Grivas led his armed rebellion to achieve union with Greece – 'Enosis'. Tensions were high. We were wearing civilian clothes by that time. I shall always remember our coach to the hotel in town being stopped, suddenly to be boarded by a fully armed soldier of the Middlesex Regiment who pointed his rifle at us and barked "Hands up! Don't move!" A moment of shocked silence until the tension was eased by a Lancastrian voice from the back bleating "Shut the door, mate. It's bloody cold". I have a second memory too of Nicosia airport. Soon after we took off the next day, a plane parked on the airfield was blown up by Grivas's men. Thankfully we had already left and were not affected by that incident. However another problem emerged.

Ever since we left Singapore, one of the plane's four propellers had occasionally seemed to stutter somewhat. This apparently was not seen as a problem, and we continued to fly. But then, as we flew over Crete, another of the engines also faltered badly and we made an immediate return to Nicosia for it to be fixed. We finally reached our next stop, which was Malta. A similar routine – an overnight stay in a small hotel outside the capital – but on this occasion we could enjoy three or four hours of sightseeing in the capital, Valetta.

The final stage of the flight was to Blackbushe airport in Hampshire, and from there a journey by hired coach to Woolwich barracks. It had been a most interesting experience. However my main memory of that day of our return was hearing a BBC broadcast announcer saying, "This morning the temperature here soared up into the 50s". Yes, we really had got back to Blighty!

59 Across the Pond

The United Kingdom's link with the USA is a close one, and is often referred to as the 'special relationship'. Whether this is due to the common language, the history of emigration and immigration, or the fact that we and the USA are separated only by 'a pond' is not clear. However certain times of very close emotional connection stand out.

It was October 1962. The Cold War was always a background to life in those days, with the threat of a nuclear war as the main anxiety. Then, in that month, it suddenly heightened. Some years before, Fidel Castro had taken over in Cuba and the country, very near to the USA, became a communist state. Indeed it felt threatened by the USA, which was a clear reason why Kruschev decided to provide it with a nuclear defence. When the presence of rockets was discovered by the USA, the response was immediate. President Kennedy announced that they must be withdrawn. Russia did not yield, but instead dispatched a fleet to help strengthen Cuba's nuclear shield. In retaliation the USA dispatched its own fleet, which would confront the Russian ships just a few hundred miles before they reached Cuba. The odds of nuclear war breaking out were high, and the world held its breath. One news item which I particularly remember was that Pat Arrowsmith, the then leader of the Campaign for Nuclear Disarmament (CND), sensibly fled to the south-west corner of Ireland. I was due to teach in an evening class that evening, and I was certainly not the only person who wondered whether any of us would make it back home. But as we know now, it was Kruschev who blinked first. It had been a close call.

Even more emotional was the happening just 13 months later. President Kennedy was at the height of his popularity. He had gone to the Berlin wall and announced "Ich bin ein Berliner". He had promised that an American would land on the moon by the end of the decade, and not merely circle it is as a Russian Sputnik had done. And he had won against Russia in the Cuba crisis. And then came tragedy. I recall that I had just left the office on my way to a small party when I saw the 'KENNEDY SHOT' announcement on a newspaper billboard. I had to queue to buy that newspaper, such was the impact and the shock, and I continued on my way to where I was heading. But in no way was it a party. Instead it was quiet discussion in a sober atmosphere, with no music. Very soon all present left for home, to view the television coverage with their own families. Certainly a sad day to remember.

In 1969, the promise made by Kennedy was kept. A Russian Sputnik may have been the first spacecraft to reach the moon, but it was the USA who landed the first man. Once again I recall the actual moment when we learnt. It was evening and I was with my friend Herta and one or two others. The television was switched on. We could see the open hatch of the spaceship, with steps dangling. The picture was extremely blurred, but we could make out the descent of Neil Armstrong. Then, as he stood on the moon surface he made that statement which we all know: "That's one small step for a man – one giant leap for mankind". There have been many flights since, and we now look forward to that day when we shall land on Mars. But once again it was a moment of particular closeness with the USA.

The years passed on and world affairs changed substantially. The Berlin Wall came down; the Cold War seemed much less; the Middle East took its place as the scene of conflicts. I was in my Market Answers office on that day which we all remember – September 11, 2001. The telephone rang: it was my son Adrian. "You should go home if you can, Dad, and look at the television. A plane has just hit the World Trade Center". I quickly went home, which was only five minutes away, and saw the remainder of that terrible day. A second plane hit the Towers, another hit the Pentagon, and a third crashed due to the action of the passengers. Then, as the world watched in horror, the Towers collapsed to the ground engulfed in that cloud of dust.

The special relationship between Britain and America never seemed closer than on that day. But what will the future bring, I wonder? With such issues as Syria and a more aggressive Russia, and with the presidential contest between Trump and Clinton still to be resolved as I write, one can never be certain.

60   What's missing?

C'est la vie includes much that has happened or that I have done in my 80 years, but there are clearly subjects that have not been covered. Here now are 5 of them.

Gardening. I grew up in a small house where I had almost 100 yards of garden to play in, and a father who was a keen gardener. But I was not a gardener in any way. Instead I limited myself to picking fruit from the various fruit trees and bushes, plus the occasional lawn-mowing. I must admit that it was pretty much the same in later life. For quite a number of years I lived in houses with gardens. The gardener however was not me, but my partner. What, I sometimes wonder, has gone wrong?

Cooking. Although not learning to cook nor even helping my mother with the cooking in my early days, I took my turn with the food preparation (normally of fry-ups) when in college and occasionally later on. It was a camping expedition with my children and a couple of their friends that was the turning point. I had made some simple meal on the portable stove, served it to the children in the normal way, and was met by a refusal to eat from two of them. My offering was thrown away, and the 10 year-olds cooked their own. It was then that I gave up trying. Now, at a more advanced stage, I no longer cook and certainly do not read cookery books nor look at cooking programmes. Instead I have a microwave and can call on the most amazing selection nowadays of ready meals. And of course my method saves me many kitchen-hours too.

Car maintenance. Sunday mornings were always the most popular time for this. If you ventured out of your house, you were bound to see numerous persons – almost entirely male – tinkering below the raised bonnets of their car. Whether this was a sign of manliness, or a wish to leave their partner (or themselves) in peace, I do not know. In support of that hopefully interesting pastime, there were an abundance of car maintenance evening classes. I have no regrets at not being a practitioner.

Artistry. This also is missing from these pages, but I do have regrets at having no skills whatever in drawing or painting. The almost universal advice given to parents by educationalists is to provide their young children with pen and paper to indulge in drawing. But there are some children who do not enjoy drawing, and I was one of them. Whether this was simply due to lack of skill or had any other cause, I know not, but it has continued all my life. On the other hand, I much enjoy the work of others, and have spent many hours visiting galleries and admiring the work of artists from Michelangelo to Banksy.

Social media. There is almost universal amazement that the large majority of those travelling on bus or underground train seem to spend their journey time tapping on, or simply viewing, a small screen. What on earth are they all looking at? Maybe we need a small survey. However what is certain is that the norms of the past – reading a newspaper or a book; even conversing – have greatly diminished in frequency due to social media (or 'antisocial media', as it should perhaps be renamed). The same is true in my own career path of marketing. Although the standard methods of publicity still strongly exist, the use of social media for such purposes as sales or gaining memberships has also become vital. This is perhaps best seen as a generational change. I do not doubt for one moment the worthwhileness of the vast advances that have taken place – for example, instant communication with friends or happenings on the other side of the world. I simply note that the subject of 'Social Media' is missing from these pages.

And so ......

I therefore pass on my apologies for omission from the pages of *C'est la vie* to all art teachers, car buffs, TV chefs, Gardeners Question Time listeners and Mark Zuckerberg.

61   The television era

It will be of no importance in your lifetime or mine
**Bertrand Russell (said about 'television' to BBC's
Grace Wyndham Goldie in 1948)**

It was in 1928 that John Logie Baird invented his television. Here in the United Kingdom, the first regular high-definition television service started transmission in 1936. It was shut down for the war, and the BBC resumed its service in 1946, transmitting from Alexandra Palace.

In those first few years, it was Mrs Goss who was the nearest person in our road to have a television set. It was very small, and we and other neighbours would sometimes crowd around it. My family's television came later, obviously still just a black-and-white. But as the years went on, features such as colour television and commercial channels with advertising started to emerge. It was only when snooker began to be shown that I personally bought a colour set for my parents. The main reason was that my mother had unexpectedly found a great interest in snooker. That well-known joke ('For those of you watching on a black-and-white set, the red ball is the one behind the green ball') was actually meaningful in her case.

Nowadays of course we have 24-hour television and a host of channels available, plus all the technical developments which I leave completely to others to use and understand. My own main interest remains with the BBC and I trust that this public service broadcaster, funded by a near-universal licence fee, will continue to prosper and to show the way ahead to the world.

Programming has developed greatly over the years. There was a time, before television, when the concept of the King making a Christmas broadcast caused huge consternation on the grounds that it would be listened to by working men still wearing their caps. It was a time when standing up and removing your hat for the national anthem in the cinema or elsewhere was universal. But modern ways gradually prevailed, and the monarch's Christmas message takes place. In a similar way, the decision to allow cameras into Westminster Abbey to see the Queen's coronation in 1953 was also a game-changer for television in this country.

It is impossible now to imagine a world without television although a new generation is starting to watch its TV programmes on media such as iPhones and tablets. My own day starts with listening to the news on radio, and of course it is only radio which is possible when I'm driving. However for the rest of the day, if there is a need to turn on broadcasting, I become a viewer rather than a listener. I would not dare to list all my favourite programmes or favourite personalities, though Match of the Day and some current affairs items would certainly be high in my choice.

Instead it is easier to list those that I might turn off rather than on. Heading that list would be programmes more unreal or apocalyptic in nature, such as those featuring vampires or werewolves, or possibly armies of monsters attempting to kill those more human in appearance.

Or maybe that is what the future will actually hold and I am not facing up to it.

62 Possessions are a prison

My son Adrian looked at me struggling with some archive boxes and declared "Possessions are a prison". Was he right or wrong? He was by no means the first person to express that view. Jean Paul Sartre for instance wrote "We are possessed by the things we possess". Other persons, such as monks, deliberately own no possessions and thereby – in their view – achieve freedom.

There are well-known examples of owning too much, such as Imelda Marcos, the wife of the ousted Philippines dictator. When her home was finally entered, she was found to have over 1000 expensive pairs of shoes. That story went viral in newspapers around the world. My closest experience to this – though tiny by comparison – was entering my Auntie Dot's very small flat in South London to carry out clearance. Two whole rooms were completely clogged from floor to ceiling by clothing and other items that she had barely, if ever, used. The local charity shops had a field day when they received it all.

My own house moves from occupying a whole house to just sharing my son's flat are not dissimilar. The greatest bulk was furniture, and E-Bay came to the rescue in disposing of much of it. The next greatest volume was my books, which have somehow grown to almost four thousand in number. Shelf construction has solved that space problem.

However I still have much paperwork in the flat and over 40 boxes of paperwork in storage. It is owning it, organising it and dealing with it that remains the problem.

Take owning it for example. Nowadays – and only in theory – we could live in a paperless society thanks to computers and scanners. But not having much ability in these skills nor in the art of throwing things away, I have the detritus of scores of years of keeping miscellaneous paper items.

Disposal is sometimes recommended but is not really the answer. Could I put in a skip, for instance, years of records of companies or clubs that I have formed or helped run? Or about three boxfuls of old newspapers ranging from the abdication and the first man on the moon back to some from Victorian times? Instead it is a case first reorganising and then perhaps of pruning. After all, this is only fair for my executors who, given my age, need to be taken into account.

And so in answer to Adrian's original statement that "possessions are a prison", I have to partially agree – not in the sense of owning valuable objects, but in the sense of giving me a lot of work to do. Could writing *C'est la vie* be part of the answer, I wonder?

63   Working for oneself

All but the extremely fortunate few need to live by working. However there are two basic ways of doing so. One is by being employed, whether by the State or by a commercial enterprise. The other basic way is by working for oneself. For example you could own a small shop or be a plumber. Or you could be a surgeon, an accountant or a farmer.

I was in the first category, working for employers, for 30 years, and expecting to continue until retirement. However a takeover occurred and I chose to start my own business. I will say straightaway that it was both tough and enjoyable. Tough because the responsibilities such as risking your own money and relying on your own skills (all with the safety net of next week's pay cheque missing) can be considerable. Enjoyable because you can choose your own working hours and holidays, make your own decisions and hopefully enjoy growth both of income and possibly status.

As my career until that takeover had been in marketing, the self-employed route which I chose was also in marketing. This route was to start a company called Market Answers, which specialised mainly in qualitative market research. Over time it expanded to include two partnerships (Corporate Answers and Sample Answers) plus another operation, Third Age Research. Initially I ran it from home but after a few years moved to a local business centre. One further feature was that I decided against employing my own staff, but used instead the many people and services available to me.

The work itself was highly fascinating. Qualitative research consists largely of depth interviews and focus groups, aimed at exploring issues in real depth. Presenting results and discussing issues with clients is another good source of job interest. Consider for example some of the surveys we carried out, especially in relation to financial services. What are your plans for retirement and thereafter, and why? What do companies do in the fields of sponsorship and giving to charity, and what are their motivations in doing so? One survey that we carried out over 20 years ago for a small syndicate of banks was into the financial product, PPP. Clearly it met a need. I hasten to add that it was the banks themselves, and not me and my company, who were responsible for all the selling abuses which followed!

And so in summary. Yes – I was enjoying company life as an employee and might well have become better off by that route. But I am extremely glad that I had my 15 years of doing my own thing.

64   Fun on four wheels

I was born at a time when car ownership was low. Even when I was at grammar school in the years just after the war, I recall only one pupil from my class being driven to school in a car, and my parents never owned nor drove a car. I did have 6 driving lessons, funded by my paper round, when I was in the sixth form, and then took the driving test which has been compulsory since the 30s. I failed, however, which is not too surprising since I'd had no other car to practise in.

That was how I left it, both during my years of National Service and in my three years as an undergraduate which followed. Hitch-hiking became a frequent way of travel, both in this country and on the continent, and this continued until my final year in college. Then, as mentioned elsewhere in these pages, I "married into a scooter" quite soon and stayed on two wheels for the first three years of my marriage. In the end, though, I did then have some further lessons, and took and passed the driving test. There was to be no more hitch-hiking. We bought a cheap, second-hand minivan, and my four-wheel life began.

It was when I moved from my advertising job to product management in a food company that I first had a new car. This was a company car, and it was a Ford. I could now pick up hitch-hikers instead of being one, and travel abroad as well as through England, Wales and Scotland. Just three or four years later, it was another company and another Ford – this time an estate car. By this time, I was once again single, and both for main holidays and the occasional weekend I would go camping. My estate car became quite used to European travel, quite possibly starting off in Munich (for Oktoberfest) at the end of September, then heading off to such places as Norway, Czechoslovakia or Sicily, with or without a companion.

I remember particularly one holiday with a friend from BP in Nigeria which we took in his car rather than mine. This was a Reliant Scimitar, and the reason why I remember it was because of its speed. It was in that car that I achieved my own fastest speed, which was 127 mph, on a German autobahn. Our final destination was Norway, and we returned home by boat from Bergen to Newcastle. The British motorway network had recently been extended in the north of England but few cars were yet using that stretch of the M1. Fortunately the same applied to motorway police and their cameras.

My next employer was more relaxed in the company cars which were permitted. I had much enjoyed that holiday in a Scimitar, and I was now able to have one – the more sedate estate version rather than the quicker sports model – as my choice. They were certainly happy driving days, and this was perhaps the only time of my life when I have been envied. A new employer led to a further change of car. This time it was an Alfa Romeo, smart in appearance, but unfortunately very prone to breakdowns. The only occasion when it ran really smoothly was when I took it on holiday to Italy, where it must have felt completely at home. My kind employer allowed me to switch to a Mazda, which I'm pleased to say was totally reliable.

And so to my final company car. This was a new Audi, which I was able to retain after I left the company and was running my own business for several years. Those were days of sheer comfort and reliability. In fact it was only after some 10 years and once it had reached no fewer than 160,000 miles that two or three parts needed replacing, and it was time to change.

The latest part of my four-wheel journey has been with a Honda Accord for seven or eight years, which have taken its mileage from 50,000 miles to over 100,000, including two month-long tours around European countries. I have been told more than once by those in the car business that the engine will last forever, and it seems to be happening. Unfortunately the same cannot be said for the Honda's body, and it is showing many signs of paint loss and scratches including one or two that I myself must own up to. Paradoxically that could even be an advantage since few self-respecting car thieves would be attracted to an apparently damaged car.

In the meantime driving remains one of – perhaps the greatest of – my pleasures. At my age, driving licences have to be renewed every three years, and I look forward to this continuing.

65   The accidents of life

Anyone's life is bound to have its share of accidents. After all, the statement is made that "it was an accident" each time that any of us trip or knock something over. The only hope is that one's accidents are not so serious as to permanently damage or even curtail one's life. Like any child, I suffered the normal hazards of the playground and the crop of scars from falling off a bike. Additionally I received a fractured arm from a branch breaking while I was tree climbing. But my life has included some that were more serious. I start with two home accidents and then go on to two car accidents.

The first occurred when Caroline had just learned to toddle. That morning, while our au pair's attention was temporarily diverted, she crawled into the kitchen and skilfully pulled herself up. The problem was that she pulled herself up against a stove, and was able to reach up and topple the contents of a saucepan containing almost boiling milk over her face and arms. She was whisked immediately to hospital, who did their best, though one arm remains scarred to this day. In addition Dickie, who was then a nurse, gave almost continuous loving and medical care to her daughter's face for the next two or three weeks, and no scars remain.

Adrian was a few years older when his serious accident occurred. It took place in a modern flat which had plate glass windows on the ground floor looking out onto the garden. Keen to get to the garden, he raced down the stairs and – not realising that there was glass – ran right into the plate glass window, smashing it. All one can say is that he was fortunate to escape with only minor injuries to his face and elsewhere.

Going onto my own serious accidents, the first took place in the south of France whilst I was hitch-hiking. Just before we reached Perpignan, the driver who gave me a lift was faced at the very last minute by a car in the opposite direction coming out from behind a lorry and about to smash into us head on. He skilfully took the only action possible, which was to leave the road. We crashed into a tree, amazingly breaking a branch that was about 12 feet above the ground, and of course our car was a write-off. It was the only time that I thought for a minute or two that I had died. However it turned out to be a bloodied face, largely the result of a shattered windscreen, which two days in the local hospital at nearby Thuir successfully treated. The driver himself was only bruised. In truth it was a remarkable escape. So too was the one which occurred just a few years later.

On the second occasion, I was driving my own car when it happened. Together with my friends Jim, Keith and Eddie, we had driven up from London and were just a mile or so short of the home of Jim's Auntie Betty in the Argyll village of Bellanoch when it happened. Whether it was a blowout, or simply going too fast, I shall never know, but the car overturned as we sped round a corner. Fortunately all of us

179

were able to crawl out and only Eddie needed treatment for a cut in the local hospital's A&E department. But once again, it was a fortunate escape for us, plus of course a considerable talking point for the villagers.

So what more can I say about accidents? Only, perhaps, that I seem to have been rather lucky. I just hope that this will continue.

66   The demon drink

What key will unlock the door to hell? Whis-key
National Temperance Almanac

Drink, i.e. alcoholic, has both its good and its bad sides. Good – because it can have a great taste, enhances social life, and is the result of high farming and manufacturing skills. Bad – because of its associations with over-drinking, addiction, violence, muddled thinking and waste of money. What about in my case? Let me start with some background.

I came from a drink-free home. On my mother's side, there had been a link with the teetotal Band of Hope in her childhood in the early 1900s. On my father's side, alcohol was forbidden on strict religious grounds. Even the drink in communion was certainly not alcoholic. Thus it was at the age of 14 on a school trip to Germany before I had my first taste of beer, though mainly we stuck to apfelsaft apple juice. However I did experiment, and we did visit a vineyard. I was 16 or 17 before I first visited a pub in this country. This was in Enfield, with three or four friends from school. Then, even during my National Service in Hong Kong, my drinking – which was of beer – was only occasional. In fact I barely recall any drunkenness amongst we servicemen in those days.

So I was probably at university before I ever indulged in more than one or two glasses in a single session. There were of course pubs in Cambridge, and those students who rowed were certainly amongst those who indulged heavily in drinking sessions. But it was in coffee bars, then very much in fashion, where we would meet our friends. My early memories of college include the holding of sherry parties; perhaps in the early evening; perhaps even at lunchtime. However when I became resident in college itself, boisterous staircase parties became more frequent. It was the practice for at least one of the choices available to be of different alcohols mixed together as a punch. Goodness knows what was in it. And of course there were the effects too – the inability to keep it within oneself at the time, and the hangover which followed. "Pigs!", I remember my bedder saying on one occasion, "They're all pigs!"

It was whilst working as a tourist rep in Spain during my long vacations that I first acquired some proper appreciation of alcoholic drink. Bars and nightclubs were part of the tourist routine, as were excursions to vineyards and wine distilleries. Tarragona, where I was based for most of the time, had a wine distillery, plus the distillery where the liqueur Chartreuse was produced in the summer. It was just along the coast from the area where most Spanish champagne (now called 'cava') was produced. Such skills as pouring out a bottle above a tower of six glasses, and watching it trickle down from glass to glass, was part of a rep's repertoire of skills. Also, in those days when only two or three bottles could be brought back to England, we were sometimes able to persuade a tourist to bring back an extra bottle for us.

Back to college life, I discovered that I had a greater talent than most in drinking beer quickly. In other words I could always manage to down a pint in six seconds and occasionally in five seconds. This was a useful skill. Winning a contest, or responding to a bet that I couldn't drink it in that time, brought an occasional free pint. I also discovered traditions in one or two pubs such as drinking a yard of ale. However my main memory remains those staircase bottle parties.

Once I had left Cambridge and even during the early years of marriage, the bottle party remained common. We ourselves never had any violence or really bad behaviour, though the complaints about noise and even the late at night knock on the door from a policeman was always possible. One of the great pleasures, however, became the visits to pubs such as those in the Isle of Dogs (before Canary Wharf existed), along the Thames towards Reading whilst I was a Londoner, and of course throughout Gloucestershire when I lived in the Cotswolds. But alcohol limits for driving and the breathalyser then became part of the British way of life. Necessary, certainly, but a great damper on one's night out. Another source of pleasure was that I really started to appreciate real ales, such as Youngs Special from the Youngs Brewery just over the Thames in Wandsworth, or from Wadworths and other breweries in Gloucestershire. Although never an actual member of CAMRA, I studied its guides avidly. But then it all changed.

It was some 10 years ago that my cholesterol level rose alarmingly. The very clear guidance from my doctor included switching from beer to red wine – furthermore to take no more than three glasses a day. Apart from the occasional glass of spirits or Guinness, I have followed this advice. Moreover, since retirement, I find that I am popping into one of the many coffee bars for a cappuccino rather more than into the local pub. Unless, of course, I happen to be in Scotland at the time!

Although getting tanked up before a football match is a British tradition and has given us an unfortunate reputation all over Europe (hence my use of the title Demon Drink), the drinking of alcohol is an important part of a civilised nation. Let us hope that Prohibition never arrives in this country.

67   All change!

The French say 'Plus ça change, plus c'est la même chose' (the more it changes, the more it stays the same). I do not believe that to be right. The changes that have happened in my lifetime and will take place in the next 80 years are too fundamental. The changes started by the Industrial Revolution were already advanced by the time that I was born in 1935. Take an example. There was a time when mankind was almost completely reliant on horses for horsepower. Then came the industrial advances, and the few remaining horses were already by 1935 mainly used for recreation.

Since then the change process has gone much further. Compare 1935 with 2016. For instance:

- Mobility – cars and planes have increased out of all proportion throughout the world, though unfortunately creating clogged roads, air pollution and greenhouse gases.
- Energy – we are in the process of a change from fossil fuels – coal and oil in particular – towards renewable energy methods and, most dramatically, nuclear power.
- Social – changes we have seen include a sharp decline in marriage in these post-war years, an increase in divorces, great growth in the numbers

of children born outside wedlock, women in the work force as well as men, greater sexual equality, and changes in gender acceptance.

- Technology – only a few computers existed before 1960, but it is now impossible to imagine the world without them. The same applies to the Internet and social media, both of which barely existed before 2000.

- Health – medical advances have led to many populations living 10 or even more years longer than was previously the case.

- Cities – within less-developed countries, there has been extremely large migration from the countryside and from subsistence farming to living and working in cities which may at times have several million inhabitants.

(Almost the only thing not to have changed are the aggressive feelings between many nations. It was 25 years ago that Francis Fukuyama wrote 'The End of History' announcing that the great ideological battles were now past and that liberal democracy would now be the way ahead. But the rules of Utopia seem as far away as ever)

So what about the next 80 years? Despite all the above huge changes which have taken place, there is so much more to come. In fact the speed of change is likely to be as great or even greater in the next eighty years. Here again are some examples:

- Technology – automation has already replaced huge numbers of manual and clerical jobs. Artificial intelligence will take the process further. For example, it is almost certain that robots will be, say, better surgeons and accountants than are humans
- Sustainability – possibly the greatest problem facing the world in the future is climate change and its effects. Efforts are being made to check it, but at the same time population (and hence the need for more food), greenhouse gases, and so on are greatly expanding.
- Specific instances such as medicine, where today's antibiotics seem to be approaching their end.
- Great international changes, such as the relative positions of China and USA, will have huge implications and effects.

And so, in conclusion, what will it be like in 80 years time, or even a few years earlier when King George reaches his 70s? It is natural for all of us to want heirs, but what kind of world will they have to survive in at that time? I leave it to others to reflect on that.

68   **My vote**

It was William Gilbert, the librettist partner of Arthur Sullivan, who wrote in the opera *Iolanthe*:

I always think it comical
How nature does contrive .....
That every boy and every gal
That is born into the world alive
Is either a little Liberal
Or else a little Conservative.

So what about me?

I came from a totally non-political family of Daily Herald readers. My first encounter with political parties was in the 1945 general election when I was nine years old. I remember seeing several men wearing dark blue (Conservative party) rosettes, and shouting "Up Cambridge!" as I cycled past them. They seemed rather taken aback.

My political interest started in college, partly due to the Suez Crisis and partly due to the presence there of students from many countries. Very soon I joined several clubs with political interests, such as the Federalists, the Heretics and the Bandung Society. But which political party should I join? That seemed important. My mind was made up by two factors. Firstly I heard the Liberal leader Jo Grimond speak t a meeting, and was impressed. Secondly – and probably more importantly – it was announced that the jazz musician Humphrey Lyttelton would be playing at the Liberal club's annual Green Ribbon Ball. Thus I joined the Liberal club, and thoroughly enjoyed its discussions during the ensuing next three years.

It seemed that WS Gilbert's words were being proved right in my case.

Having left college, however, my involvement dropped away. I had never been interested in politics as a career choice, but nevertheless I visited meetings of the local Liberal associations where I lived at the time on several occasions. I found however absolutely no discussion about Liberal party policy, nor indeed about any party's policies. Instead it was all about stuffing envelopes and similar. Another negative factor was that for most of my working years, the Liberal party had less than a dozen MPs in Parliament, and were certainly not likely to win in any constituency where I was then living. Thus I can truly say that my vote has always been a wasted vote under our lamentable first-past-the-post system. Nevertheless the Liberal party's views were always very close to my personal views, and I have thus remained totally loyal in my voting over the years.

Then came the time of growth, leading in 2005 to the Liberal Democrats winning 57 seats and joining in coalition with the Conservative government. They certainly played their part well, both in ensuring that there was an effective government and in their influence on numerous policies such as, for instance, the pupil premium. But as we now know to our cost the British public, having no experience of the necessary compromises which take place in coalition government, turned against the Liberal Democrats and pushed them back to only eight MPs at the next election.

So what now for the Liberal Democrats?

Clearly the political situation is extremely uncertain. On one hand there are all of the issues following the Brexit decision. I have always been a keen supporter of the European Movement, so that decision disturbs me greatly. And then there are all the issues affecting the Labour Party leadership and hence the nature of any effective opposition. How best, if at all, could the Liberal Democrats act to improve their position? There is certainly no easy answer. Fortunately, as a Londoner, I'm able to easily visit those meetings which quite frequently take place in 'Westminster Village' to discuss such issues.

And of course my vote will always remain as it has been since I came of age.

69   Travelogue

The world is a book and those who do not travel only read one page

St Augustine

Travel has always been a major interest of mine, even though only twice outside Europe. Quite a number of my jaunts abroad are written about in these pages. It's time to pull it all together.

What started it was that my father was a railwayman, and the families of railwaymen were entitled to two free passes a year and privilege tickets for their other rail travel. Of course there was no travel outside Britain, and restrictions on various coastlines within Britain, in the war years of my youth. Nevertheless by the time I finished primary school in 1950, I had already travelled widely, including my first time to Scotland. I remember that particular trip well. We stayed with Charlie Barker who had sold his hardware shop in Potters Bar and moved up to Arbroath. The highlight for my father was going out in a fishing trawler all day from five in the morning until five in the afternoon, sharing in all the fishermen's work including in the hold, and not being sick. A highlight for me was that, for the first and only time in my life, I wore a kilt for a day.

My rail travel continued through my early grammar school years. For example we had an excellent family holiday in Barmouth in North Wales, and I journeyed with my father and brother to John O'Groats and around the Isle of Skye. I also started touring on my own, joining the Youth Hostel Association as a young cyclist and developing a liking for the hills.

It was in 1950 that I first went abroad. This was a school exchange visit to Frankfurt-am-Main. The remains of the war were only too evident, but the welcome was great and I made friends for life. Then in 1951 came my cycle trip to Normandy and Paris with a friend, Roy, and in 1952 my first visit to Spain which included a three-week rail tour that included Madrid and Andalusia.

In 1954 came the three-week journey by troopship (still my only cruise) to Hong Kong for 18 months of my two-year period of National Service. We were of course restricted just to the colony and the nearby Portuguese island Macao. However whilst carrying out my duties with a military theodolite in the New Territory hills, I was able to see across the frontier to China itself.

Once demobbed, I spent three months in each of Paris and Madrid, brushing up my French and Spanish ready for studying them at university. Then, once at Cambridge, I was particularly fortunate to be in the right place at the right time with the right language to become a travel rep in those very first years of the package tour industry. Additionally, it was with university friends that I made my first of half a dozen trips to the Munich Oktoberfest.

Travel outside the British Isles unfortunately never figured at all during the whole of my career. Nevertheless it continued as a mainstay of my life, but always as a tourist. For example I had to wait until marrying before I went to Ireland. My first visit was to stay with a friend in Dublin, then continue south-west to kiss the Blarney Stone. A year or two later, my second visit was to stay with other friends in Belfast, plus a trip across the border to Donegal. I should mention too that, in a later part of my career, my company was due to be taken over by the Bank of Ireland, and I had to make several visits by both air and then by train to Dublin and Belfast.

Over the years that followed, my travel in Europe continued every year or every two years. Sometimes this was with family, such as trips to stay with close friends and also relatives in Toulon, Paris, Switzerland and Germany. I must include my two honeymoons – both of which were partly spent in Granada. Talking of Spain, we even owned a house for several years in an 'urbanisation' a few miles south of Alicante. But all these trips with partner or family were only part of my travel experience. During my single years, three weeks of camping in September and October formed my normal holiday. Several times I started off by two or three days in Munich's Oktoberfest but then went on – perhaps to Sicily – perhaps to Norway and Denmark – or perhaps even behind the Iron Curtain to Hungary, Czechoslovakia and East Germany.

193

It was in 2002 that I first met my friend Mark Covell who, as I recount elsewhere in these pages, had been one of the victims of severe violence by Italian police at the Genoa G8 demonstration. Battered into a coma and unable to be employed for some years, he eventually received very large compensation. However this required fairly numerous visits to Italy, in which I quite often accompanied him. It was also in those post-2000 years that I attained senior office in my speaking organisation, which required considerable travel at weekends to various parts of England, Wales and Scotland.

All this brings me up to the most recent three years which in many ways have seen the most exciting adventures of all. Two of these were driving trips around parts of Europe, one of five weeks and one of four weeks. The first, which I refer to as my Christmas Card Safari, included driving through 14 large and very small European states, overnighting with people on my Christmas Card list, some of whom I had not seen for 30 or 40 years, and also revisiting some of my very favourite places such as Venice and the Amalfi coast in Italy. The second such tour, just completed, was around Spain and Portugal and included my first ever visits to Compostela and to Gibraltar, three days with Portuguese friends getting to know the Lisbon area for the first time, and of course calling in at Granada – but not on honeymoon this time.

The third adventure was totally unexpected, and was magical in the extreme. This was an invitation to take part in a debating training mission to that African country which suffered such a horrifying genocide a generation earlier – Rwanda. Certainly an amazing experience and also one to a country that is now full of hope. (By the way, the stories of these three recent journeys are on my website.)

So that is an account of my travels – so far. It took longer than expected, and some of the special parts are described elsewhere in these pages. I certainly feel myself fortunate, even though I have failed to cross the Atlantic or go to any of those countries on the other side of the world such as Australia and New Zealand.

For 2017, I am torn between two possibilities. One would be a summer car trip to Scandinavia, crossing the Arctic Circle, then heading across via Finland to St Petersburg (calling on Father Christmas on the way!), and returning back home via the three Baltic states and the north of Germany. The other, also a summer car trip, would be driving down the Danube to the Black Sea, doing some touring in Greece, then returning back home via Serbia.

But there will still remains one regret. In my younger years, I had only a single travel ambition in life. That was to see and preferably walk upon Mount Everest.

70   **What to wear**

The first thing the first couple did after committing
the first sin was to get dressed.
Thus Adam and Eve started the world of fashion,
and styles have been changing ever since

Time, 8 November 1963

One of the discussions in a brief debate the other day was whether, if it was cold, to put on more clothing or more central heating. The logic here in the UK is to choose more clothing: perhaps to return to those days when we had separate summer clothing and winter clothing. More heating would mean higher bills and – in a wider context – more need for energy in the world. And yet the opposite is often the case. Some people, whether through lack of thought or simply to impress, wear totally unsuitable clothes and then complain "I'm really freezing".

Clothing is clearly an important part of everyone's life, so here is my own contribution.

The main issue for boys in those early days was at what age we switched from short to long trousers. 12 or 13 seemed to be the average age in the 50s but now it is younger and always by the time that secondary school starts. Then too I get the impression that more adults now return to shorts during the summer, and the old sensitivity about knobbly knees is forgotten.

Fashions for uniforms still seems the same, whether we are talking about Boy Scouts, soldiers, trainee baristas, or plumbers. However we have definitely moved on from that daily march – entirely of suited males, often with bowler hats, – across London Bridge to the City. (Trilbies were always non-U). Wearing a tie, too, has become less mandatory for many, even for some television presenters. Lord Reith must certainly be howling in his grave.

Regardless of these general moves in style, my life has also seen more temporary fashions. Teddy Boys, for instance, started in the 50s and flourished for a time. Then, in the 60s, the Mods took over and, mounted on their scooters (still without helmets in those days), challenged the primacy of the motorcycling Rockers. The various hippie styles followed soon after and further fashion trends have appeared ever since. Hair style has been completely subject to trends. One of my own strongest National Service memories is of new recruits' well-groomed haircuts being close-cropped on their first or second day of arrival at camp, and the distress it caused. Back in civilian life and helped by the emergence of the Beatles, short hair gave way to much longer hair for a period, though partly replaced eventually by the skinhead movement. Then, to bring us right up to date, we have seen the return of the beard in its various formats for the first time since they were laughed out of existence by the cries of 'Beaver!' shouted out by the Bright Young Things of the 20s. What is true of the male sex is of course certainly also true of the female sex. The British fashion industry has grown amazingly during my own life. The wartime austerity dresses were very quick to give way to the New Look in the 50s. The length of dresses was always an issue varying over the years from longer gowns to knee length skirts and to hot pants. Hats meanwhile seem to have disappeared completely except at Ascot. A more private memory is of an evening in the swinging 60s when I remember my work colleague John Bingham and I accompanying a topless young lady to the Establishment Club, and none of us being stopped or arrested. But probably the primary difference has been the almost complete change from skirts and dresses to slacks and trousers which has accompanied the move by women from staying in the home to the outside working world.

So how have I adjusted to the changing scene? There was little scope for personal differences as one progressed from short to long trousers and then to army uniform for National Service. A little scope existed at university. For example I, like nearly every student, had my duffel coat which is perhaps best described as an early version of today's hoodie. Then came the office world which required me to wear a suit until those final years when I became my own boss.

My hobby of participating fully in speakers clubs was just as bad. "Be sure to button up your jacket" was the Number One instruction to aspiring speakers throughout the country, especially in Scotland, until fairly recent years, when a sweater or just a shirt has become equally popular in many clubs. But of course the dinner jacket tradition (with kilts *de rigueur* in Scotland) still holds much sway.

One of the most interesting developments in recent years has been brought about by newcomers to this country. I find it a sheer delight to see the colourful saris, the full Muslim dress, the tall Jewish hats and of course the Caribbean influences such as Rastafarian hairstyles. All these have made for a more varied and less constrained country. Long may they continue.

And as for me? I have not changed my own style for many years – with two exceptions. One is that I no longer need to style my hair. The other is that I have changed to a more voluminous size of shirt. And of course my naturist occasions, always very few in number, have certainly ceased for ever.

71   Fatherhood continues

Young families frequently split up, and mine was one of them. I remained in our family house while the children and their mother Dickie moved to North London. It was quite an eventful time. Dickie carried on with her new life though troubled at times with ill-health, the children adapted to new surroundings, and I myself continued to be in close contact with the children.

Their first new home was with Dickie's friend Paddy, her husband Louis and their two daughters in Muswell Hill, North London. Dickie had taken up market research interviewing after the children were born at the suggestion of Paddy, who was already following that course with the firm Motivation Analysis. It was a positive period. The children started attending a go-ahead Montessori nursery school, whilst I became a frequent visitor. Paddy and Louis eventually moved away to a cottage by a small river in a village in far off Cardiganshire where I visited them once or twice and was particularly fascinated to see actual coracles being used for fishing on the river. Dickie meanwhile moved to a different flat in Muswell Hill and then to one close to East Finchley where once again I was a frequent visitor, quite often babysitting for a full night. Sleeping has never been a problem for me. Indeed I was prone to sleep very deeply indeed. For example it was at about 2 AM one night that the police broke into the flat where I was (meant to be) babysitting the children. The reason was that they had been crying. The worried neighbours had knocked but had no answer, and so – presuming that the children had been left on their own – contacted the police.

Dickie moved again, this time to the Golders Green house of (Professor) Bob Green, another person whom I had known for some time. He was the owner of the market research practice Motivation Analysis and also at this time the first Professor of Psychology at the recently formed Open University. Bob's house, entitled Dragon's Moon, was a magnet for highly interesting people, some of whom I remained close to for many years. Once again the children adapted well into the new life.

There were several further changes to come. These even included a period, some time later and after our eventual divorce, when my ex-wife and I shared a house, along with two or three lodgers and, of course, with our children. Perhaps I shall write a longer story of those years of 'fatherhood at a distance' some time, but shall leave it at that for now.

It is a sad fact that many marriages fail, but it happens. I continue to feel that it is better in nearly every case for the children to remain with the mother. However it is far better for the father and especially for the children if the father remains in fairly close contact. Dickie and I set out to achieve that and, to a large measure, I believe that we succeeded. But all that is now very many years ago.

72   Albie

What makes a friendship? Is it meeting someone with a similar background to yourself? Does it arise through having similar views and interests? Neither of these apply to my friendship with Albie. But it has been a long and loyal relationship.

I first met Albie when I was about 30 and he was five or six years younger. I was living in Fulham at the time, newly separated, and with a vacancy for another tenant. Albie, who was flat-sharing nearby, fitted the bill. He was a fairly typical Londoner, born and bred in Fulham and now earning his living as an electrician. He moved in and the friendship began. He introduced me to one or two of his favourite pubs and to some of his friends, and I gradually began to learn more of his background. I found out that a few years previously he had had certain problems with the law and indeed had spent a year or possibly more within the confines of Brixton prison. I learned too that some of his friends had had a similar history. However those days were behind him and made no difference to our relationship.

There was perhaps just one problem, which was his feeling that he was being targeted. At times this was more serious and he became particularly defensive and paranoid. For example his feeling that our next-door neighbour was targeting him caused him to erect a kind of shelter in his room. However this also made no real difference and when I moved house to Shepherd's Bush, he too moved with me and continued as my lodger. I was particularly grateful for his help with a bathroom and shower and some rewiring, and life went on peacefully.

There were just one or two slight changes. For example, Albie had always backed the horses, but gradually spent more time on this and less on his electrical work. But this was in no way a problem since it actually provided an income. His method was straightforward. He would spend much time studying the stated odds offered in the pages of newspapers, and from time to time identified odds being offered that were clearly erroneous. These might be few in number, but they provided an income and not a loss.

During this period between marriages, my holidays were a great source of pleasure. These were normally camping holidays, starting in the middle of September and lasting for about three weeks . The first port of call on several occasions was the Munich Oktoberfest. Albie and I shared one particularly enjoyable holiday together. From Munich we drove down to Sicily and explored particularly Palermo and the west coast around Trapani. It was on the journey back through Italy that I discovered for the first time the Amalfi coast and the Island of Capri.

Eventually I remarried and moved to Cheltenham. From time to time Albie visited, and our friendship continued. However by this time another oddity was taking place. He had always sought to hide that Brixton part of his life and therefore occasionally used a different name. He was now using, I believe, four names for the different parts of his life, such as betting, banking and applying for work or non-work benefits. Naturally we talked very little about this but it did seem to be proving advantageous for him financially. Finally he was in a position that he had long sought, which was to live abroad in warmer weather and in a totally free manner. His chosen venue was southern Spain, not in the Costas, but close to the Portuguese border.

I see little of Albie these days, and occasionally miss him. He has been a good friend and his way of life, very different from mine, is not my concern. I'm occasionally asked why he and I are good friends. After all, our background and our interests are so different. How can I answer? As I acknowledged at the start, friendships are made on various grounds. Perhaps having a similar background. Perhaps having similar interests. Or perhaps just by accident. It is the final one which applies in the case of Albie and me.

73   **The reunion**

It is always a great pleasure to get together again with a group of old friends or colleagues. I meet some friends of 30 years standing at the annual conference of my Speakers Club association, whilst the Biddulph Bash, as some call it, is a lunch where several persons known to each other for even longer meet up each year. Then yesterday I went to a gathering where several of those present first met 50 years ago. It was a most enjoyable reunion.

The occasion was the 'open day' being held by my friend Jim Ferguson to celebrate his 70th birthday. Having passed 80 myself, my birthday card to him said simply 'Happy Birthday, young'n.' We first met back in the 60s. My wife and I had split, she and the children had moved out, and I was left with an empty house and mortgage. The answer was to find tenants. Jim and 2 or 3 of his ex-school friends moved in, and thus began several years of fun and friendly life. The term 'The Swinging Sixties' was not an exaggeration. Yesterday was a chance to renew old times with some people from those days.

How do such reunions work? Firstly by catching up with each other's lives. For instance, there were civil engineer Steve and wife Cathy, Coulsdon residents of many years. Also present were ex-advertising design man Alan and his wife, Tessa, now living near Hailsham in Sussex. I remember them all before they married, and now they were retired. Jim's sisters were there too. Linda, who was there with her husband and one of their daughters. And Lorna whose married and family life had been far more complex.

Reunions work too by conversing about those old days. These events included – embarrassingly for me – the time that I overturned my car en route to Jim's Auntie Betty in Argyllshire, with Jim, Steve and another friend, Eddie, in the car. Another memory from those days was that Jim himself was engaged in the process of 'coming out' with a friend. This was less easy in those days, especially with the family dominance of 'Big Jim', his father. Tragically his friend died, and Jim suffered greatly.

Photographs always help, and we were able to flick through a collection from Jim's babyhood to the present day. His early career was in civil engineering work in Algeria and, of course, his flatmate of those years, Roger, was also present. Jim went on to be deeply engaged in Channel Tunnel construction, while his career thereafter included long periods in foreign countries such as Libya and Vietnam, and even opening a bar in Ibiza. However his real fulfilment was in meeting Francesco and settling down with him for a happy life. Thus the reunion that we held yesterday was more cosmopolitan than simply a meeting of good friends from the 60s. Indeed, when we came to the cutting of the birthday cake which his sister had made, it was necessary to for us all to try singing our

'Happy Birthday' chorus to Jim…James…Jacques…Jaime…
Giacomo…Santiago three times and in three languages.

The ability to make and retain close friendships is one
of Jim's great strengths, and yesterday was proof of this.
During these last two or three months, I have been engaged
in thinking about the past years of my own life. The writing
of memoirs is quite a lengthy business. But yesterday's
'open house' occasion was like memoirs in a different form,
viz that of chatting. Not written down – but very much alive.

74   Conferences

We all attend conferences, just as we may attend Dinners. They may be annual or one-off, to do with our work or some other interest, and for a single day or longer. All of them have needed much organising. And quite frequently over the years that has been largely my responsibility. So what has been involved? Perhaps I can give some examples from my own experience.

My marketing career was bound to include some organising of sales conferences. Take for example one that I organised at the National Conference Centre near Birmingham in the 80s for the launch of a new financial services product. As always I and my team had the standard tasks, which were primarily

- to book the room and date and – for some attendees – book rooms overnight
- to liaise closely with the venue on issues such as timing, decor, and props
- to fix a programme of speakers, and brief them as necessary
- to arrange for technical support, which included showing the TV commercial
- and to liaise with the sales force regarding their full attendance.

I have always tried to add to something 'extra' or unexpected. On this occasion it was to agree to inviting George Brown, MP and Cabinet member, to come along and give a speech. He duly arrived and, despite seeming slightly unwell (I nearly said 'sozzled'), his speech was excellent and – as we found out from the debrief – much appreciated.

A great interest of mine since the 80s has been the Association of Speakers Clubs, or ASC for short. In my time there, I have held several offices and have been quite frequently involved with the organisation of special meetings, dinners, and conferences. The example I have chosen was ASC's national conference held in a Watford hotel in 1999, attended by over 200 members and partners. Creating a planning team, fixing its meetings and logging its progress always applies, and the task included too:

- involvement in selecting and visiting venue and accommodation
- overseeing the 'chief steward' position, i.e. the link with those running the contests, the workshops and the dinner to ensure everything worked smoothly everything to do with attracting and then booking the 'bums on seats'
- planning the social side, including a 'Cockney evening' and an outing for members' partners (On this occasion it was a visit to Hatfield House), getting local ASC clubs fully committed and volunteering to assist

It was a guest who provided the main 'extra' on this occasion, viz the Mayor of Watford who turned out to be a delightful and quite young lady. Not only did she attend the Dinner, but unexpectedly led the dancing until about 1.30 in the morning, completely charming all those who were still surviving until that time.

And one final conference – a current one. The Sylvans, the Cogers and London Debating are about to hold their 7th annual debating conference in Eastbourne. This is a weekend with 3 styles of debating, 2 workshops, an Annual Dinner and of course much socialising. As always the organising job includes:

- the booking and liaison with the venue
- the financial arrangements
- publicising the event and attracting the delegates
- ensuring that all the props and other presentation needs are present
- plus all the paperwork of programme printing, joining instructions, menu choice and so on.

So will it be successful? As always with conferences, you plan to the best of your ability – and then you keep fingers tightly crossed!

75 The cash in your pocket

Finance is a factor to be reckoned with throughout the whole of life. It largely determines what the government will do or will not do, and this applies to individuals too. So here are some reminiscences about money from my own life.

There was not too much money around in my own family. I recall that my father used to give the whole of his small railway signalman's wages to my mother, who returned some of it to him as pocket money. I recall too that my bus ticket to the next town, Barnet, which was 3 miles away, used to cost me a penny halfpenny in my primary school days. The farthing still existed but had no real use by then. However the penny had its value, as the expressions "penny for the guy" and "pee for a penny" both show.

Pocket money existed for, say, a twopenny ice cream. However my relation with money only really began when, at the age of 12 or 13, I started doing a paper round. Initially I earned three shillings and sixpence (3/6) a week for my labours, though this gradually rose.

It was also during my secondary school years, at the age of 14, that I went abroad for the first time on a school trip to Frankfurt in Germany. This introduced me to pfennigs and marks and also to the concept of currency exchange.

An interesting fact in those early post-war days, before exchange rates had settled down, was that it was sometimes possible to make a tour of four or five countries, changing money at each border, and actually increase the sum that you had started with.

I was 18 when I started my two years of National Service. As an army 'Gunner' (i.e. a Private), my pay was 24 shillings a week, though this increased to 30 shillings after six months. Then came University. Those were the years in which the State used to pay students for attending university, rather than the reverse. Some of the costs still stick in my mind. For instance, the fine levied by the proctors for being out after 10.30 PM was six shillings and eight pence, i.e. one third of a pound. Another memory concerns the amount of money that one could take abroad, which was just £25 per person at that time. So some of us devised (in fun, I should say) a rent-a-baby scheme. If you were going abroad, you would rent a baby at Dover (and thus could have and take an extra £25 to spend), drop it off in Calais, pick it up from there when you were on your way back, and return it finally to Dover.

At the time I was leaving university, back in 1959, my career aim was to reach the income level of £3000 per year within 10 years, which would be comfortable, and if possible attain £4000 per year thereafter. But one has to start somewhere, and my own first job – which was in an advertising agency – brought me £550 per year.

It was in 1963 that I bought my first house. This was in Fulham, then still a downmarket area, at a price of £5000. I remember borrowing £500 from an aunt to use as a deposit, much to my mother's displeasure! However I also needed to find some part time work to help pay our way, and a local pub – the Peterborough on Parsons Green – provided the answer. I still remember some of the prices. For example a pint of beer cost the customer one and tenpence halfpenny in the public bar and one and elevenpence halfpenny in the saloon bar.

In 1967, I moved to a job as a Product Manager in Associated Biscuits Ltd. One of the product manager's roles was to decide the price of each of our products. My time in the company coincided with the United Kingdom's change to decimal currency. Small price increases were fairly normal, but decimalisation gave the opportunity for extra benefit. The secret was to pitch our packet prices at levels which would then benefit further from rounding up (instead of rounding down) when the new currency started. As an example, increasing a packet's price from 1/8 to 1/9 , i.e by 5%, seemed a reasonable step. With decimalisation, however, it was then rounded up to 9p, thus effectively giving us a 12½% increase in the year in total! Although never openly stated, I believe that this practice certainly contributed to the rise of inflation to nearly 15% in the one or two years following decimalisation.

I shall leave my reminiscences at this point as we start to get onto modern times. Naturally my own earnings increased as my career advanced, as did the price of houses and of everything else in the world. Money has changed its format too. The jingle of cash in one's pocket is no longer a sign of wealth – rather the reverse, in fact. With the coming of credit and debit cards, the cheque book is becoming out of date and the first voices are being heard even prophesying the end of cash. Luckily I still retain some coins from those younger days. However I can buy nothing with them, and their only value now is to a numismatist.

76 Fanfare

This interesting part of my life started at the very end of 1993 and lasted for over 10 years. Jim Johnston, who had founded Horsham Speakers Club which I was attending, had come up with another idea. This was to give a large boost to the Horsham District's arts scene and culture by having a Horsham & District Arts Festival. Over a drink, he invited me to chair an Open Meeting on the subject. I did so, and the meeting of about two dozen people, mainly from arts groups and the Council, agreed the concept. I found myself as Secretary and, soon afterwards, local resident Sir Michael Checkland, ex-Director General of the BBC, agreed to be our Executive Chairman. Jim's idea was on its way!

First meetings of committees are always similar. Members' roles are confirmed, aims and principles are decided, finances are agreed, and so on. Horsham's District Council and also Sainsbury's would provide the initial funding. The festival would be held two-yearly, starting in June 1995, and running for 10 days. It would be a combination of professional and amateur activity, seeking to cover all the arts if possible, and would spread across the District's towns and villages.

Arts Fanfare, as it became named, was successful from the outset, with 70 events scheduled for the 10 days. It started with an open air performance by the Marching

Band of the local Christ's Hospital ('blue coat') School, and the scene was set. On the 'professional' side, that first year included a concert by the Bournemouth Sinfonietta Orchestra, an open air performance of Macbeth at Bramber Castle by the Factotum Theatre Company, and the Pimlico Opera performing Rigoletto. On the 'amateur' side, participation by local groups was very high indeed. We were able to enjoy entertainments that ranged from a jazz concert on a Horsham bandstand to various art and even pottery exhibitions, plus a wide range of singing, dancing, instrumental and literary events in towns and villages throughout the District. I personally chaired some items, such as an evening devoted to Shelley who was born locally, and Fanfare's first Macmillan Lecture, given on this occasion by Oleg Gordievsky, who was interviewed by Lord Bethell. The speaker was the highest ranking KGB officer ever to be recruited by the British, and his book "Next Stop Execution" had just been published.

Following the success of its first year, Arts Fanfare continued along its two yearly schedule, with a Fanfare Weekend also taking place on two of the intermediate years.

Excellent musical events by the Royal Philharmonic Orchestra, some opera companies, and others were always in the programme, whilst non-classical performers such as Cleo Laine and Jools Holland also came and delighted us. The district's most well-known venue – The Capitol in Horsham – was joined by school and village halls and other meeting sites throughout the area for evenings of poetry or music, a variety of exhibitions, and various lectures and workshops. Imposing events such as a Hilaire Belloc day at Shipley Windmill close to where he lived, and an Arnold Bax weekend were included along with more exclusive opportunities such as the chance to see the newly-carved Stations of the Cross in a small parish church.

I stayed on as Minutes Secretary but also took over as Literature Coordinator when Jim Johnston sadly found himself unable to continue. These were exciting years for me in a largely new and unknown field. My aim was to include 10 spoken items, or possibly more, in the 10-day arts festival. I was able, for instance, to enlist the attendance of more well-known figures such as Colin Dexter (the creator of Detective Morse) and local playwright and writer Simon Brett for such occasions as the regular Macmillan Lecture. Terry Waite and Benjamin Zephaniah were two of those who agreed to speak and present the prizes for the schools writing contest sponsored by Horsham's Royal & Sun Alliance. The numerous other inclusions in the programme included talks or workshops by the district's excellent writing and poetry groups, performances for children by storytellers, entertainments and even monologue contests by Jim Johnston's own Muse and Music Society, and so on.

Local cooperation was always forthcoming, as indicated perhaps in this letter which I wrote to Professor Stanley Wells, possibly Britain's leading Shakespearean, when he was coming to address us in the charming South Downs village of Steyning. The words of my letter included:

"basically it will be you (plus your colleague) discussing Shakespeare, his legacy, your book, any questions – with a refreshment interval halfway and the book signing at the end. However, if you think it would add to the evening, there is scope for more, and I can provide you (if you wish) with piano, pianist, singer or reader for poetry, play or prose".

Horsham Arts Fanfare came to a close following our 2005 festival. The reason was a mixture of (i) some main contributors being unable to continue further and, (ii) more significantly, budget reductions. It had certainly brought great pleasure (and many good friends) to me and hopefully too to the people of Horsham and its District. It was I believe also in that year that the development works which had been taking place to the Capitol in Horsham finally came to an end. The occasion was sealed by a visit by the Queen and Duke of Edinburgh, to which I and my partner Judy, along with the other Fanfare committee members, were among those invited. In retrospect, this was perhaps a fitting conclusion to 10 excellent years.

77 Panaputti

I f you are in a club or Institute for long enough, you may well find yourself eventually at its helm for a year. But what happens thereafter? Do you simply become a has-been? Or is there something else to look forward to? The Association of Speakers Clubs (ASC) attempted to solve this problem 25 years ago by organising the 'Panaputti Club' for its Past National Presidents and their partners. (Why that name? Because it includes the letters 'Pa', 'Na' and 'P'.) The club has only one activity, which is to meet annually for a delightful weekend.

It was in 2008 that I handed over the ASC Presidency to my then Vice-President, Joe James, and thus became qualified to attend this annual get-together. Each year it follows a simple pattern. One or two volunteers will decide on a location, select a hotel, and make the weekend's arrangements. We meet up on Friday, visit a local attraction and hold the Panaputti Dinner on Saturday, and depart on Sunday. There are only two rules. One is to wear the purple tie gifted to Past Presidents; the other is not to talk about ASC (which is impossible!).

The Panaputti weekend has a special place for me, because it gives the opportunity to once again spend time with people who have become close friends. However my reason for including it in *C'est la vie* is to briefly mention some of the locations and excursions which have taken place. There was a weekend in Durham for example. In its own right Durham is a city to enjoy as a sightseer. However we added to this an excursion to the museum town of Beamish which gave us an opportunity to visit a colliery and an old tram system, and to experience what life was like over a hundred years ago. Other special venues have included Edinburgh, where the excursion was by open-top bus to the now-decommissioned Royal Yacht Britannia, and to Lytham St Annes on the Lancashire coast, which included both a tram ride in lit-up Blackpool (the event always takes place in October) and a coach trip to see the attractive developments that had taken place in the Liverpool docks.

From a touristic point of view, a location which I particularly enjoyed was our weekend in Ayrshire in Scotland in 2014. Our Saturday excursion was to the new Robert Burns Heritage Centre located by his birthplace further down the coast. I was particularly interested because the Italian patriot Garibaldi was feted in the poet's 100th anniversary celebrations which took place in 1851, and I am very fortunate in having an inscribed book of poems presented to Garibaldi on that occasion.

This year, 2016, we stayed at Grantham in Lincolnshire, and marvelled at the historic Belton House nearby, which played an important part in the abdication of King Edward VIII. And our location next year? We wait to hear!

78   **Hey Jude!**

Well, actually her name is Judy, but our first meeting dated from that time in the 60s, when I was eking out my money by teaching Spanish in a Dulwich adult evening class. Among my 7 or 8 students that year was Judy, who was about my own age. Our friendship grew quickly, although we took it no further in those married days.

It was 25 years later that we met again. I was visiting a speakers club in Kent and was introduced by name. The interval arrived and a lady sitting behind me asked, "Did you use to teach Spanish?" The friendship returned – this time more strongly since both Judy and I had both experienced marriages, parenthood, and divorces. In my case, I had lived in the Cotswolds and had now returned to living and working on weekdays in London. In Judy's case, she had moved to Canterbury and had become a senior figure within the Social Services world. In fact she had the been a leading pioneer in what is now the common practice of people receiving care being encouraged to determine their own care needs and to control their budget accordingly. Thus eventually began a dozen years of spending most of my weekends in Kent. I hold many memories. Here are just a few.

One obvious memory is of Canterbury itself, a city which has played such a large and important part in British history.

Tourists flood in, especially from the continent, to admire the cathedral and the city walls. There is much else to wonder at also, such as the extensive remains of the St Augustine Priory, bearing the name of that original Christian missionary to this country. Then, a few years after we re-met, Judy moved a few miles to the picturesque village of Wickhambreaux. Once again this was a place with a long ancestry, a beautiful though much smaller church, and a small river to remind us that Thanet long ago was an island separated by water from the rest of Kent. I have fond memories of long barbecue days in Judy's cottage garden whose upkeep was a much loved pastime for her. I got to know also many other parts of East Kent, such as .... the town of Whitstable with its history of oysters .... Broadstairs and Margate, with their close links to Charles Dickens and the painter William Turner respectively .... the Cinque Ports from time past, especially Rye and Sandwich .... and of course today's ports of Dover and Folkestone. Then there were other delightful places to visit too – none more delightful than the Aspinall Foundation's Howletts Wild Animal Parks, home to so many animals and with great achievements in conservation.

Another memory is of Judy's family – a son in Western Australia where I too had a stepson at that time – a daughter in a mountain village in the French-speaking canton of Valais in Switzerland – and another daughter, living in Lincolnshire, but then moving to carry out duties in a castle in the glorious Dee Valley between Aberdeen and Balmoral.

Many of our journeys were around Britain, often to speakers club dinners and conferences and at other times to stay with Anne-Marie, her daughter. We travelled abroad also. I recall for example a delightful Eurostar rail trip with Judy to attend my cousin Theresa's birthday celebration in her home near Paris, and another holiday where we enjoyed the delights of Andalusia. However that Spanish tour was badly marred when Judy was violently mugged in Madrid and had to be repatriated back to this country for hospitalisation. Even more tragic were the last visits which Judy made to Switzerland, which were to provide help and comfort to – and finally attend the funeral of – her eldest daughter. I am glad that I was able to be with her for some of those terrible days.

As I mentioned at the start, our separation finally came about – Judy to develop a new life for herself – and me to continue my established London life. But, as the French say, 'C'est la vie', and those Kentish years were certainly a most positive part of my life.

79   **School years**

Are school years the happiest years of a person's life? Maybe yes. Maybe no. Another question – are they the most important years of a person's life? That, I believe, is more likely. Of course much has changed over the years. My school years were in the 40s, my children's were in the 70s, and my grandson's spanned the millennium. Many schooling issues are still being discussed and some earlier decisions reopened. However here are some of my personal memories.

I started in Ladbroke Primary School at the age of five. Nowadays it is more normal to attend nursery or kindergarten before that age, but few existed back in the 40s. Another alternative might have been preparatory school, perhaps commencing there at the age of seven, but the cost of private schooling was not possible for my family, even if it had been wanted.

Classes were from Class 6 for the youngest to Class 1 for the oldest. All teachers were female (it was, after all, wartime) and most classes had about 50 pupils. This high number never seemed to affect the teaching, and all but a handful of us went on to grammar school after the 11+. Some of the happenings come back easily into the memory, for example the singing, playing and drawing or painting which were the stuff of Miss Levy's infant class when I first arrived. Of course we also learnt to read!

Other items that I remember well include ..... the occasional wail of the local air raid siren, causing all of us to leave our classrooms and go quickly into the Anderson shelters built into the playground. ..... the occasional tests we had, in which I always tried to beat Heather Phillips who was normally top of the class ..... and that time when Valerie Clifton asked, "Who came bottom?", and was roundly told off for asking the question.

Then came the 11+. I can only speak myself, but I do not recall it causing general anxiety. Virtually everyone in the class had decided to go on to grammar school rather than to Parkfield which was the local secondary-modern school, or even to the one local Technical School, and the great majority of us duly did so.

I followed my older brother to Enfield Grammar School, which was 6 miles from Potters Bar. At first I travelled by bus, but after a year or two changed to cycling. The school was first founded, right next to the parish church, in 1558 and one or two of the very early buildings still existed. It was for boys only, but Enfield County School, which was for girls, stood 50 or 100 yards away. Some 700 pupils attended, broken down each year into Upper A, Lower A, Upper B and Lower B. The Upper Sixth and the Lower Sixth forms were divided into arts and science. The war had now ended and all teachers apart from two were now male.

Whether or not present day schools are different I do not know, but for the record our progress included:

- taking French in year one
- adding German or Latin in year two
- giving up art and woodwork from year three (optional)
- also – an option which I took – giving up Science (chemistry, physics, biology) from year three and continuing just with arts subjects

A small group of us were also able to start Spanish as an extra language in the fifth form, which suited me greatly.

Most left school after the fifth form, leaving a fairly small number to continue our schooling. Something that always pleased me was that we were given more freedom in the sixth form, such as free lessons or permission to work in the local library.

It was in my first week in the Lower Sixth that I learnt possibly my greatest lesson. The teacher was Doc Collins, known to us best for his chain-smoking and hence stained beard. I wrote a French essay and presented it to him. He started reading, then mentioned "There is a mistake here", and a minute or two later "There's another mistake". On finding a third, he threw my essay back to me and said that, as I was now a sixth former, I should not insult him by giving him unchecked work. It was at that point that I realised that it was I – and not the schoolteachers – who were responsible for my future progress. That was a valuable lesson indeed.

80   **On reaching 80**

It was many years ago that I gave up birthdays. Hopefully I remembered those of others, and helped celebrate them – but not mine. Thus it was my offspring (can you call people in their 50s "children"?) who decided that my 80th was somehow different and needed recognition. And so it became something of a milestone. For me, however, it was rather a pause for reflection in an ongoing story. I possessed numerous records and reminders accumulated over the years, but what had really stood out? This book has been an attempt to answer that question.

There are of course many incidents which have been omitted, especially through forgetfulness. For instance:

- those days when I visited my children, who were then studying in the excellent but completely vegetarian St Christopher School in Letchworth. Their first request when I visited was always to be taken out to a Wimpy bar
- that time (long ago, I hasten to add) when I slept off a heavy night's drinking on a stranger's doorstep, and was loudly screamed at in the morning
- even that occasion when I first attended a divorce court, and the thought crossed my mind that it would make an excellent site for a wife-swapping party.

There may indeed be further episodes of *C'est la vie* still to come.

However my main reflection concerns the good fortune that has been my lot in life. It is much more than health and longevity, though these play a part. In particular I was deeply moved by the strength of those people who overcame their severe disabilities to seek to reach the podium in the recent Paralympics.

I have to be deeply thankful:
- to the parents who gave me encouragement to study and full freedom to explore and do my own thing
- to the schools and university which I attended
- for the choice (marketing) which I made for my working life which meant that I looked forward to work every day rather than putting up with it
- for the interests and hobbies which have continued to enthrall me
- for the warmth and friendship which I have received from so many people
- and most of all to my families and those dearest to me

This book, *C'est la vie*, has been my attempt to write down many of the happenings. One day perhaps you will write down your own story.

80 + 1 Looking ahead

I am disappointed. I was planning to finish inscribing these 80 elements of my 80 years within my 80th year. But it has been a busy year and many other things have happened. So now here I am, at the age of 81 and one month, still writing.

Let me look forward rather than back. Reluctantly I have to concede that 81 is old age. To quote the American comedian, George Burns, *"First you forget names, then you forget faces. Next you forget to pull your zipper up and finally you forget to pull it down".*

Of course there could be quite a number of years still to come. It was recently reported that the planet's oldest male – aged 113 and living in Israel – marked his birthday by celebrating his Bar Mitzvah which he had somehow missed about a hundred years ago. But realism and the mortality tables which were part of my everyday life when I worked in life assurance, suggest something different. So what are my intentions for the next 5, 10 or 15 years?

Recent happenings, including the Paralympic Olympiad in Rio, have led to much discussion about employment prospects for the disabled. Perhaps we oldies are similar. Life has moved on. We are well past the days when retirement at, say, 55 or 65 largely equated to the end of one's activities. Instead it is seen as the start of a new life. We are even past those days when becoming 70 represented old age. 80 is now more likely. So my own main intention is very definitely to continue with my normal activities such as speaking, debating, U3A courses, and using my driving licence and Freedom Pass to the full. In addition a very small bucket list remains. It includes further trips to Ireland and Italy and perhaps one to Scandinavia also, though my initial life aim of viewing Mount Everest has regretfully dropped out of the bucket.

There is one additional activity to fit in. A lifetime of working and of hobby interests, much of it in pre-computer days but still continuing today, has naturally resulted in extensive amounts of paper records (as well as some 3800 books). In addition my several house moves before becoming a flat-dweller have given rise to some 40 archive boxes in storage. Thus one of the activities which necessarily has to be added is a considerable amount of sorting.

And so I look ahead with anticipation. There remains much to do. Indeed I may need to update *C'est la Vie* in a few years time.

www.gwynredgers.com

Lightning Source UK Ltd.
Milton Keynes UK
UKOW06f1142030917
308472UK00001B/40/P